Family Circle ABZ's of Cooking

Edited by Lucy Wing with
The Family Circle Food Department

Volume 2

Introduction

Break bread with us in this volume which is dedicated to the baker and includes recipes for all your favorites—biscuits, blueberry muffins, old-fashioned yeast breads, easy yeast breads, quick breads, brownies, and much more. There are recipes for leftover breads, such as thrifty stratas and bread pudding, plus creative ways to use frozen bread dough available in the supermarket. You'll learn the basic facts about bread baking, and about ingredients—what flour to use; the difference between dry and cake yeast. With this volume as a guide, bread baking is easy and fun.

Also included are almost instant dishes you can create with an electric blender, plus tips on using this versatile appliance. When you have to watch your purse strings, try one of our budget-trimming main dishes. Entertaining is a breeze when you follow our complete menus for a Mexican or Chinese-style brunch or a lovely spring buffet. For a grande finale, try a luscious blueberry or blackberry dessert, or a show-stopping ice cream bombe.

The abundance of information and taste-tempting recipes contained in this volume are guaranteed to expand your cooking knowledge and bring enjoyment to all.

Contents

Cover photo: Sesame Potato Twist Loaf, page 91;
Steamed Ginger Brown Bread, page 95; Honey Wheat
Bread, page 91

ISBN 0-8249-9002-1

Copyright ©MCMLXXXII by The Family Circle, Inc.
All rights reserved.
Printed and bound in the United States of America.
Published by Ideals Publishing Corporation
11315 Watertown Plank Road
Milwaukee, WI 53226

Family Circle Staff

Project Editor	Lucy Wing
Food Editor	Jean Hewitt
Senior Associate Food Editor	Jane O'Keefe
Art Director	Joseph Taveroni
Copy Editors	Karen Saks
	Susan Tierney
Project Management	Annabelle Arenz
	John Jaxheimer

Ideals Publishing Staff

Project Editor	Julie Hogan
Food Stylist	Susan Noland
Photographer	Gerald Koser
Project Management	James Kuse
	Marybeth Owens

Photographs by: Avedis, Paul Christensen, Joseph Heppt, Richard
Jeffery, Allen Lieberman, Bill McGinn, Rudy Muller, George
Nordhausen, Gordon E. Smith, Bob Stoller, Rene Velez

BISCUIT In the United States, the word "biscuit" is used to describe a small, soft, unsweetened cake, considered a quick bread, made from baking powder or soda-leavened dough and served as a hot bread. It was in the late 1700's that these little cakes first appeared here in place of traditional yeast breads. They became popular because they were so quick and easy to make.

Our biscuits are not found in other parts of the world. In fact, the word is French in origin for flour-made cakes that were baked twice to dry them out for use on long trips. The English call sweet biscuits, cream biscuits or water biscuits what Americans term cookies or crackers.

To make tender, flaky biscuits, handle the dough as little as possible. If you want biscuits with soft sides, bake them in a small round pan with the sides of the biscuits touching. Refrigerated ready-to-bake biscuits and packaged heat-and-serve biscuits are readily available today. See also **BREAD, Quick.**

BAKING POWDER BISCUITS

Bake at 450° for 12 minutes.
Makes 12 biscuits.

  2 cups *sifted* **all-purpose flour**
  3 teaspoons baking powder
  ½ **teaspoon salt**
  ¼ **cup vegetable shortening**
  ¾ **cup milk**

1. Sift flour, baking powder and salt into a large bowl.
2. Cut in shortening with a pastry blender until mixture resembles cornmeal. Preheat oven to 450°.
3. Add milk; stir lightly with a fork until a soft, puffy dough forms.
4. Turn out onto a lightly floured surface. Knead lightly about 20 times.
5. Roll or pat dough to ½-inch thickness. Cut into 2-inch rounds with a floured biscuit cutter, working neatly from rim to middle so there will be few scraps to reroll. Place biscuits, 1 inch apart, on an ungreased cookie sheet.
6. Bake in a preheated very hot oven (450°) for 12 minutes or until golden brown. Serve immediately.

Drop Biscuits: Prepare Baking Powder Biscuits, increasing the milk to 1 cup. Drop by spoonfuls, 1 inch apart, on ungreased cookie sheet. Bake following Biscuit directions.

Sesame Butter Fingers: Heat oven to very hot (450°). Melt ¼ cup (½ stick) butter or margarine in a 9×9×2-inch pan. Put ½ cup sesame seeds on a large plate. Prepare Baking Powder Biscuits. Roll or pat dough to an 8-inch square on a lightly floured surface. Cut square in half. Cut each half into nine 4-inch strips. Dip each strip into the melted butter, then dip one side into sesame seeds. Arrange strips in 2 rows in the baking pan.

Bake 15 minutes or until golden brown.

Scones: Prepare Baking Powder Biscuits, but do not add the ¾ cup milk. Instead, add 3 tablespoons sugar, 1 teaspoon grated orange rind and ½ cup raisins to dry mix. Beat 1 egg with ⅓ cup milk; pour into dry ingredients. Stir and knead as in Biscuits. Divide dough in half. Pat each half to an 8-inch circle. Cut each circle into 6 wedges. Brush tops with milk; sprinkle with sugar. Place wedges, 1 inch apart, on ungreased cookie sheet. Bake in a very hot oven (450°) for 10 minutes or until golden brown.

Cheddar Biscuits: Prepare Baking Powder Biscuits and roll dough out to a 12×8-inch rectangle. Place twelve ½-inch cubes of Cheddar cheese about 1½ inches apart in 3 rows of 4 each, on half of the dough. Fold other half of dough over to make a second layer. Cut between cubes of cheese into twelve (about) 2-inch squares. Place on greased cookie sheet. Bake following Biscuit directions.

Mini-Herb Biscuits: Prepare Baking Powder Biscuits but stir 1 teaspoon dry mustard and 1 teaspoon Italian herb seasoning mix into flour-shortening mixture. Add milk; knead and roll dough into a 10 × 6-inch rectangle. Cut into 1-inch squares. Place on ungreased cookie sheet. Bake following Biscuit directions.

BUTTERMILK BISCUIT SQUARES

Bake at 450° for 20 minutes.
Makes 24 biscuits.

    3 cups *sifted* all-purpose flour
    3 teaspoons baking powder
    ½ teaspoon baking soda
    1½ teaspoons salt
    ¾ cup vegetable shortening
    1⅓ cups buttermilk

1. Sift flour, baking powder, baking soda and salt into a large bowl.
2. Cut in shortening with a pastry blender until mixture resembles cornmeal. Preheat oven to 450°.
3. Add buttermilk; stir lightly with fork until a soft puffy dough forms.
4. Turn out onto a lightly floured surface. Knead lightly about 20 times.
5. Transfer dough to a large, ungreased cookie sheet. Roll out to a 12 × 8-inch rectangle. Cut into 2-inch squares. Separate slightly, about ¼ inch apart.
6. Bake in a preheated very hot oven (450°) for 20 minutes. Dust lightly with flour. Serve hot or at room temperature.

RALEIGH BUTTERMILK HAM BISCUITS

Bake at 450° for 10 minutes.
Makes about 22 biscuits.

    1½ cups lightly spooned
        all-purpose flour
     2 teaspoons baking powder
     ½ teaspoon baking soda
     ¼ teaspoon dry mustard
     ⅛ teaspoon salt
     4 ounces peppered ham
        luncheon meat, finely chopped
     7 tablespoons butter, melted and
        cooled
     ¾ cup buttermilk

1. Preheat oven to 450°. Combine flour, baking powder, baking soda, mustard, salt and ham in a medium-size bowl. Stir in 4 tablespoons of the melted butter and the buttermilk with a fork until the dough is moistened and clings together. Knead the dough on lightly floured surface 8 to 10 times.
2. Roll out dough to ½-inch thickness. Cut with a 2-inch floured biscuit cutter. Place on ungreased cookie sheet, 1 inch apart.

3. Bake in a preheated very hot oven (450°) for 10 minutes or until biscuits are well risen and golden brown. Remove from oven to wire rack; brush tops with remaining melted butter.

———————— •●● ————————

BISQUE This term refers to a thick, rich cream soup, usually made with shellfish or fish. Originally, the word was used for a poultry or game puree.

SHRIMP AND TOMATO BISQUE

Makes 8 servings (about ¾ cup each).

    ½ cup water
    ½ teaspoon salt
    ½ pound frozen shelled and
        deveined shrimp
     1 can condensed tomato bisque
     1 can condensed cream of
        shrimp soup
     1 pint half-and-half
     2 tablespoons dry sherry

1. Bring water and salt to boiling in a large saucepan; add shrimp. When mixture returns to a boil, cover and simmer 2 minutes or until shrimp turn pink. Lift shrimp out with slotted spoon; chop finely on a board.
2. Add tomato bisque and cream of shrimp soup to liquid remaining in saucepan; bring to boiling. Stir in half-and-half, sherry and shrimp; heat just to boiling, but do not boil.

LOBSTER BISQUE

Makes 8 servings.

     1 medium-size onion, chopped
        (½ cup)
     ½ cup (1 stick) butter or
        margarine
     ¾ cup all-purpose flour
     2 cans condensed chicken broth
     ¾ cup dry sherry
     2 cans (about 6 ounces each)
        lobster or crab meat, drained
        and diced
     3 cups light cream or
        half-and-half
     2 tablespoons tomato paste
        Salt and pepper to taste

1. Sauté onion in butter in a large saucepan. Stir in flour; cook until bubbly. Gradually stir in broth; cook until thickened. Stir in sherry and lobster. Cover; simmer 15 minutes. Stir in remaining ingredients; heat.

BLACK BEANS Also called turtle beans, these small, oval beans have a purplish-black skin with a creamy white interior. They are traditionally served with rice, but can also make a delicious soup. They are widely used in the southeastern United States, in South America, in the Caribbean Islands and Puerto Rico. For more information, see **BEANS**.

CUBAN BLACK BEANS AND RICE

One of the traditional favorites throughout the Caribbean, this dish is finding new popularity stateside.

Makes 8 servings.

     1 pound dried black beans or
        pinto beans
     9 cups water
     3 teaspoons salt
     1 pound pork shoulder, cubed
        (1 cup)
     2 tablespoons vegetable oil
     1 large onion, chopped (1 cup)
     2 cloves garlic, minced
     2 large green peppers, halved,
        seeded and sliced
     1 teaspoon ground coriander
     ½ teaspoon pepper
     1 cup uncooked long-grain rice

1. Pick over beans and rinse under running water. Combine beans and water in a large kettle. Bring to boiling; cover kettle; boil 2 minutes; remove from heat; let stand 1 hour. Return kettle to heat; bring to boiling; add salt; lower heat and simmer 1 hour or until beans are firm-tender.
2. Brown pork cubes in vegetable oil in a large skillet. Remove with slotted spoon and stir into beans. Simmer 30 minutes.
3. Sauté onion and garlic in pan drippings until soft; stir in green pepper. Cook, stirring constantly, 5 minutes; stir in coriander and pepper. Stir mixture into kettle. Continue cooking 30 minutes longer or until pork is tender.
4. Press some of the black beans against the side of kettle with a wooden spoon to mash slightly; stir in rice. Cook, stirring occasionally, 30 minutes or until rice is tender and mixture is dry. Spoon into a heated serving platter and garnish with sieved hard-cooked eggs, if desired.

Black Beans

SPEEDY SPANISH BLACK BEAN SOUP

Makes 6 servings.

- 1 **large onion, chopped (1 cup)**
- 1 **clove garlic, peeled and crushed**
- 2 **tablespoons bacon drippings, butter or margarine**
- ¼ **teaspoon ground coriander**
- ¼ **teaspoon leaf thyme, crumbled**
- ⅛ **teaspoon leaf marjoram, crumbled**
- 2 **cans (16 ounces each) black beans (do not drain)**
- 1 **can condensed beef broth**
- 3 **tablespoons sherry**
- 1 **hard-cooked egg**
- 1 **tablespoon frozen chopped chives**

1. Stir-fry onion and garlic in drippings in a large, heavy saucepan 3 to 4 minutes until soft. Add coriander, thyme, marjoram, beans and broth. Simmer, uncovered, stirring occasionally, about 10 minutes. Stir in sherry and simmer 1 to 2 minutes.
2. Meanwhile, cut hard-cooked egg into halves. Scoop out yolk and press through a fine sieve; coarsely chop egg white.
3. Ladle soup into bowls. Scatter chopped egg white over each serving, then sprinkle a little sieved egg yolk on top of the whites and chopped chives on the yolk.

BLACK BEAN SOUP

Makes 8 servings.

- 1 **pound dried black beans**
  Cold water
  Ham rind and/or bone
  OR: 2 to 3 ham hocks
- 1 **onion, sliced**
- 1 **carrot, quartered**
- 2 **celery stalks, quartered**
- 1 **bay leaf**
- 2 **whole cloves**
- ⅛ **teaspoon mace**
- 1½ **teaspoons salt**
  Dash cayenne to taste
- ½ **cup dry sherry**
  OR: 1 tablespoon vinegar
- 2 **hard-cooked eggs, finely chopped**
- 1 **lemon, thinly sliced**

1. Pick over the beans and wash well. Place in a bowl, add cold water to cover to a depth of 2 inches above the beans and soak overnight.
2. Next day, drain the beans and place in a kettle. Add 8 cups (2 quarts) fresh cold water.
3. Add ham rind, bone or ham hocks, if used, onion, carrot, celery, bay leaf, cloves, mace, salt and cayenne. Bring to boiling; cover and simmer 2½ hours or until the beans are tender.
4. Pass the vegetables and all but 2 cups of the cooked beans with all the liquid through a food mill or sieve. Return pureed mixture to the kettle.
5. Add remaining 2 cups whole beans and sherry or vinegar and bring to boiling. Serve in bowls or soup plates garnished with chopped egg atop lemon slices.

——————— ●●● ———————

BLACKBERRIES Commonly found in most of the Northern Hemisphere, these berries grow wild on long, prickly stems (canes) along the edge of woods and in fields. The shrubs are also called brambles. The purplish-black berries are plump when they ripen in late summer and early fall. When picking wild berries, you should be able to easily detach the fruit from the stem.

Today blackberries are cultivated in many states and in England. They are often eaten with sugar and cream, in pies, cobblers and puddings. Use them to top cereal or tarts, and to make jams, jellies, brandy and liqueurs. When they become too soft, mash them and cook with sugar, cornstarch and a little lemon juice to make a dessert sauce or ice cream topping. An extra plus: Blackberries are a good source of vitamins A and C, calcium and iron.

Buying and Storing: Supplies in the market from May through August are almost all from cultivation. Oregon, California, Washington, New Jersey and Michigan are some of the primary producers. Look for pint or ½-pint containers of bright, plump, firm berries. Check to see there are no stains on the containers—which indicate crushed or bruised fruits. The berries should be free from dirt or any adhering caps and from mold or decay. Soft berries are overripe; red blackberries are hard and underripe. Use within 2 days. Store unwashed in the refrigerator.

To Prepare: Wash in a bowl of cold water just before using; do not soak berries. Use your hands to gently lift them out of the water to avoid crushing them. Drain on paper toweling.

BLACKBERRY BUCKLE

A coffee-cake-style dessert dappled with soft blackberries and covered with a thin crunch of sugar.

Bake at 350° for 45 minutes.
Makes 6 servings.

- 1⅔ **cups** *sifted* **all-purpose flour**
- 1¾ **teaspoons baking powder**
- ½ **teaspoon salt**
- ½ **teaspoon ground cardamom**
- ¼ **cup (½ stick) butter, softened**
- ¾ **cup sugar**
- 1 **egg**
- ½ **teaspoon vanilla**
- ⅔ **cup milk**
- 2 **cups frozen unsweetened blackberries (from a 1-pound bag), thawed and drained**
- 2 **tablespoons sugar**
  Whipped cream

1. Sift flour, baking powder, salt and cardamom onto wax paper.
2. Beat butter and the ¾ cup sugar in a medium-size bowl until creamy. Beat in egg and vanilla until smooth and light. Preheat oven to 350°.
3. Add milk alternately with flour mixture to the butter and sugar, beating just to blend thoroughly.
4. Spread less than half the batter in a buttered 9 × 1½-inch layer cake pan. Sprinkle with half the berries. Spoon remaining batter evenly over the berries; smooth with a spatula. Sprinkle with remaining berries, then top with the 2 tablespoons sugar.
5. Bake in a preheated moderate oven (350°) for 45 minutes or until center springs back when lightly pressed with fingertip. Cool slightly on wire rack. Serve warm with whipped cream.

BLACKEYED PEAS Also known as "blackeyed beans," blackeyed peas are the seeds of a legume which grows on a vine. In the South, where they are grown extensively, the fresh peas are sold in their pods or shelled. In other parts of the country, you can buy them dried. People in India, China, the Caribbean Islands and Africa also cook blackeyed peas.

You can use them in soups or create bean dishes. A favorite Southern New Year's Day tradition is to serve a dish of "Hoppin' John," consisting of the peas cooked in water with bacon and rice. See also **BEANS**.

HOPPIN' JOHN 'N' HAM
Cook 35 minutes in a pressure cooker.
Makes 8 servings.

- **1 pound dried blackeyed peas**
- **1 shank-end smoked ham (about 4½ pounds)**
- **1 medium-size onion, diced (½ cup)**
- **2 teaspoons salt**
- **¼ teaspoon pepper**
- **3 cups water**
- **2 cups uncooked long-grain rice**
- **1 bunch green onions, trimmed and sliced**

1. Pick over peas and rinse under running water. Soak peas overnight in water to generously cover (about 6 cups); drain. To quick soak: Combine peas and water in a large kettle. Bring to boiling; cover kettle; boil 2 minutes; remove from heat; let stand 1 hour. Drain.
2. Combine peas, ham, onion, salt and pepper in a 6-quart pressure cooker; add the 3 cups water, being sure all peas are covered.
3. Secure cover, following manufacturer's directions; cook at 15 pounds pressure for 35 minutes, following manufacturer's directions. Remove cooker from heat and allow pressure to drop of its own accord (about 10 to 15 minutes).
4. Meanwhile, cook rice, following label directions.
5. When pressure has dropped, remove cover. Place ham on carving board and cut off skin and fat. Cut into thick slices.

6. Add cooked rice to peas, tossing to mix well; spoon onto a heated deep platter; top with ham slices; sprinkle onions over top.

COUNTRY PORK AND BLACKEYED PEAS
Makes 4 to 6 servings, plus meat for another meal.

- **1 pound dried blackeyed peas**
- **1 smoked pork picnic shoulder (about 7 pounds)**
- **Salt and pepper**

1. Pick over peas and rinse under running water; place in a medium-size bowl. Add water to cover; let stand overnight; drain. To quick soak: Combine peas and water in a large kettle. Bring to boiling; cover kettle; boil 2 minutes; remove from heat; let stand 1 hour. Drain.
2. Place pork in a kettle; add water to cover. Heat to boiling; cover. Simmer 1½ hours.
3. Add peas to kettle; cover. Simmer 1½ hours longer or until pork and peas are tender. Remove pork from kettle; trim off skin and fat; slice about half of the pork ¼ inch thick.
4. Season peas to taste with salt and pepper; spoon onto a deep large platter; arrange pork slices over top. Wrap remaining pork and chill for another use.

BLACK WALNUT This species of walnut (*Juglans nigra*) is native to the Midwest and has quite a distinct flavor. A dark, round, rough, hard shell surrounds dark kernels that are smaller in size than a regular walnut's. The shell is so difficult to crack that black walnuts are usually sold shelled. They are most often used in cakes, pies and cookies. For more information, see **WALNUT**.

BLACK WALNUT CHESS PIE
Bake at 375° for 45 minutes.
Makes one 7½-inch pie.

- **1 unbaked 7½-inch pastry shell**
- **½ cup (1 stick) butter, softened**
- **1 cup sugar**
- **3 tablespoons flour**
- **⅛ teaspoon salt**
- **3 egg yolks**

- **1 small can evaporated milk (⅔ cup)**
- **1 teaspoon vanilla**
- **½ cup chopped black walnuts**

1. Prepare pastry shell; chill. Preheat oven to 375°. Beat butter and sugar in a medium-size bowl until well mixed. Add flour, salt, egg yolks and evaporated milk. Beat with rotary beater until well mixed. Stir in vanilla and walnuts. Pour into unbaked shell.
2. Bake on lower shelf of a preheated moderate oven (375°) for 45 minutes or until center is almost set but still soft. Cool thoroughly on wire rack.

BLANCMANGE Originally a French dessert, this white pudding was almond flavored and gelled in a decorative mold or pan. The time consuming recipe involved grinding almonds with water to make almond milk, then adding sugar and a gelling agent and molding it in a pan. Today, blancmange refers to a sweet milk-based pudding, thickened with cornstarch or arrowroot and flavored with vanilla, chocolate, coconut, fruit or nuts.

CHOCOLATE BLANCMANGE
Makes 6 servings.

- **1 cup sugar**
- **⅓ cup cornstarch**
- **¼ teaspoon salt**
- **3 squares unsweetened chocolate, cut up**
- **3 cups milk**
- **1½ teaspoons vanilla**

1. Combine sugar, cornstarch, salt and chocolate in a medium-size saucepan; gradually stir in milk.
2. Cook over medium heat, stirring constantly, until chocolate melts and mixture comes to boiling and is thickened. Boil 1 minute. Remove from heat; stir in vanilla. Pour into a 3-cup mold. Cover with plastic wrap; refrigerate until cold, about 3 hours.
3. When ready to serve, run a knife around top; dip mold *very quickly* in and out of hot water. Cover with serving plate; turn upside down; shake gently; lift off mold. Garnish with whipped cream and maraschino cherries, if you wish.

Blanquette

BLANQUETTE A stew of either veal, lamb or chicken made by boiling cubed meat in a seasoned liquid rather than first browning the meat in fat. The meat is then removed and the cooking liquid is reduced and/or thickened with egg yolks and cream. Small mushrooms and white onions are usually added.

BLANQUETTE DE VEAU
(Creamy Veal Ragout)

Makes 8 servings.

- 5 pounds breast of veal
- 1 onion studded with 6 whole cloves
- 1 bay leaf
- 1 carrot
- 1 celery stalk
- 1 parsley sprig
- 2 teaspoons salt
- ¼ teaspoon pepper
- 8 cups water
- 6 tablespoons butter or margarine
- ½ pound fresh mushrooms, quartered
- 6 tablespoons flour
- 1 cup heavy cream
- ½ cup milk
- ½ cup dry white wine
- 1 teaspoon salt
- ¼ teaspoon pepper
- 2 cups cooked carrots, cut into chunks
- 16 small white onions, cooked
- 2 tablespoons chopped fresh dill
  OR: 2 teaspoons dillweed

1. Combine breast of veal, onion studded with cloves, bay leaf, carrot, celery, parsley, the 2 teaspoons salt and ¼ teaspoon pepper in a large kettle. Add water.
2. Heat to boiling; lower heat; cover kettle. Simmer 2 hours or until veal is very tender.
3. Cool veal in broth; then refrigerate until fat rises to top and hardens; discard fat. Remove meat from bones and cut into cubes. (You should have about 4 cups.)
4. Melt butter in a large saucepan; lightly sauté mushrooms.
5. Stir in flour and cook 2 minutes, stirring constantly. Combine 2 cups veal broth (save remaining broth to use in soups or stews), heavy cream, milk and wine in a 4-cup measure; stir into saucepan. Cook, stirring constantly, until mixture thickens and bubbles for 3 minutes. Season with the remaining 1 teaspoon salt and ¼ teaspoon pepper.
6. Add veal, carrots, onions and dill. Heat through.

— ●●● —

BLENDER WIZARDRY With the flick of a switch, you can transform a few leftover egg yolks into a delicious mayonnaise or turn chocolate bits into a velvety mousse. That's not magic, but the speed and power of an electric blender.

Blenders were first used in soda fountains for making malted milk drinks, appearing in the early 1930's in Wisconsin. Later the mixers were used to puree fruits or vegetables. Eventually, they gained wide usage in bars and restaurants, where frozen daiquiris and other drinks were served.

It wasn't until the mid-1950's that the blender came into its own as a home-kitchen appliance. By the late 1960's, sales soared with over sixty companies manufacturing blenders in many models. Although the number of today's manufacturers producing blenders has decreased, the versatility of the product remains.

A blender can coarsely chop nuts; mix salad dressings; make cheese or meat spreads for crackers or sandwiches; grate onions, carrots or coconut; puree cooked or raw fruits and vegetables for baby foods, special diet foods, soups and drinks.

Although the blender is a versatile food-processing appliance, most will not do such mixing tasks as whipping cream or potatoes, grinding large amounts of raw meat or crushing whole ice cubes—some companies sell attachments for these tasks.

Tips on using a blender:
- Be sure the base rests firmly on a countertop or table and that the container is placed firmly in the motor base. The lid must be securely in place before starting the machine.
- Do not overload the container—for thick mixtures, fill it ½ full; for thin mixtures, ⅔ full.
- If you're blending hot foods, cool slightly.
- If you're blending liquids with solid food, always put enough liquid in the container first to cover the blades.
- Do not overblend. Blending takes seconds, not minutes. Stop and check a few seconds after starting.
- Use a long, thin rubber spatula to scrape the inside of the container. Stop the blender completely before scraping or removing foods.
- Cut firm foods into small pieces. To grate or chop vegetables, first add enough water to the container to cover the blades; then add a few small pieces at a time. Process until desired texture is reached; drain.
- If the motor is sluggish on a certain speed, switch to a higher speed, if possible, or stop and scrape the sides of the container.
- Do not remove the container from the motor base until the blades have come to a complete stop.

Tips on cleaning the blender:
- Clean the container by filling it halfway with warm water. Add a few drops of liquid detergent. Cover and blend on low speed. Rinse and dry thoroughly. Or, if the blades are removable, disassemble and wash by hand or in dishwasher.
- Before cleaning the motor base, unplug the electrical cord from the outlet. Wipe base with a damp cloth and dry. Never immerse it in water.

BUTTERMILK SWIRL

Makes about 3 cups or 2 servings.

- 2 cups buttermilk
- 2 large bananas, peeled
- ½ cup wheat germ
- 4 teaspoons honey
  Strawberry preserves
  OR: Partially thawed frozen strawberries

1. Combine buttermilk, bananas, wheat germ and honey in container of electric blender. Cover. Whirl until smooth.
2. Pour a small amount into 2 large glasses, alternating with spoonfuls of preserves or strawberries to swirl.

Pictured opposite (left to right): Pineapple Nog, page 74; Cucumber Smoothie, page 75; Buttermilk Swirl, page 72.

Blender

FOOLPROOF HOLLANDAISE SAUCE

Makes ¾ cup.

- **3 egg yolks**
- **2 tablespoons lemon juice**
- **¼ teaspoon salt**
- **½ cup (1 stick) butter, melted (keep hot)**

1. Rinse container of electric blender with hot water. Add egg yolks, lemon juice and salt. Cover. Whirl to combine.
2. Remove lid; pour in hot butter gradually with motor still on. Whirl until sauce thickens, about 30 seconds.
3. Pour into small bowl and keep warm over hot water, if not using immediately.

APRICOT YOGURT FIZZ

The apricot yogurt mixture can be blended ahead and refrigerated.

Makes about 3½ cups or 2 servings.

- **1 can (16 ounces) apricot halves, drained**
- **1 container (8 ounces) plain yogurt**
- **2 eggs**
- **⅓ cup instant nonfat dry milk powder**
- **½ cup club soda**

1. Combine apricot halves, yogurt, eggs and dry milk powder in container of electric blender. Cover; whirl on medium speed until smooth.
2. Pour into 2 large glasses; add club soda to fill glass. Serve immediately.

PINEAPPLE NOG

Tropical in taste, an invigorating way to start the day.

Makes about 4 cups or 2 servings.

- **1 can (8 ounces) crushed pineapple in pineapple juice**
- **4 eggs**
- **½ can (8¾ ounces) coconut cream**
- **1 cup skim milk**
- **⅛ teaspoon ground nutmeg**

1. Combine pineapple, eggs, coconut cream, milk and nutmeg in container of electric blender. Cover; whirl until smooth.
2. Pour into 2 large glasses; sprinkle each with additional nutmeg.

BLENDER CHEDDAR-BEER DIP

Makes about 3 cups.

- **1 package (8 ounces) cream cheese, cut into cubes**
- **¾ cup milk**
- **¼ cup beer**
- **8 ounces sharp Cheddar cheese, cubed**
- **1 clove garlic, cut up**
- **3 medium-size dill pickles, cut up**

1. Combine cream cheese and milk in container of electric blender; cover; blend at high speed 10 seconds.
2. Add beer, Cheddar cheese and garlic; cover; blend until smooth.
3. Add pickles; cover; blend for 3 seconds.
4. Place in a serving bowl; chill. Serve with vegetable sticks or potato and corn chips, if you wish.

TOMATO SUNRISE

An eye-opener for tomato juice lovers.

Makes about 3½ cups or 2 servings.

- **2 cups tomato juice**
- **1 cup canned beef broth**
- **3 eggs**
- **⅛ teaspoon liquid hot pepper seasoning**

1. Combine tomato juice, beef broth and eggs in container of electric blender. Cover; whirl on medium speed until frothy.
2. Add hot pepper seasoning to taste. Serve immediately.

ORANGE EGG CREAM

This is especially good when the ice cream is just melted.

Makes about 4 cups or 2 servings.

- **2 cups orange juice**
- **⅔ cup instant nonfat dry milk powder**
- **2 eggs**
- **1 pint vanilla ice cream**

1. Combine orange juice, dry milk powder and eggs in container of electric blender. Cover; whirl on medium speed until smooth.
2. Add ice cream; whirl just until blended. Pour into 2 large glasses. Serve immediately.

PINEAPPLE CREAM

A quickie—makes a creamy dessert.

Makes 6 servings.

- **2 envelopes unflavored gelatin**
- **⅓ cup sugar**
- **1 can (8¼ ounces) crushed pineapple in heavy syrup**
- **1 can (6 ounces) frozen lemonade concentrate**
- **1 cup heavy cream**
- **1 cup crushed ice**

1. Combine gelatin and sugar in container of electric blender. Heat pineapple with syrup to boiling; add to blender all at once. Cover. Blend on high until smooth.
2. Add frozen concentrate, cream, then crushed ice. Blend until completely smooth. Pour into 6 serving glasses. Chill until ready to serve, about 15 minutes.

MUSHROOM AND LEEK SOUP

Makes 8 servings.

- **1 pound mushrooms, sliced (4 cups)**
- **1 bunch leeks, white part only, sliced (2 cups)**
- **½ cup (1 stick) butter or margarine**
- **¼ cup all-purpose flour**
- **1 teaspoon salt**
- **¼ teaspoon white pepper**
- **3 cans (13¾ ounces each) chicken broth**
- **1 cup light cream or half-and-half**

1. Sauté mushrooms and leeks in butter in a large saucepan or Dutch oven until tender, about 5 minutes. Stir in flour, salt, pepper and 2 cans of the chicken broth. Cook, stirring constantly, until mixture comes to boiling. Lower heat; cover; simmer 20 minutes.
2. Remove from heat; cool slightly. Pour mixture, a little at a time, into container of electric blender; cover; whirl until pureed. Pour into a large bowl. When all the soup is pureed, return to saucepan.
3. Add remaining can of chicken broth and the light cream; heat until thoroughly hot. Garnish with whipped cream and chopped parsley, if you wish.

CUCUMBER SMOOTHIE

Tangy, smooth and refreshing.

Makes about 3 cups or 2 servings.

- 1½ cups (12 ounces) vanilla yogurt
- 1 tablespoon honey or to taste
- 1 medium-size cucumber, halved, seeded and cut into chunks
- 3 eggs

Combine yogurt, honey, cucumber and eggs in container of electric blender. Cover; whirl on medium speed until smooth.

LEMON BLENDER MAYONNAISE

A winner with seafood salads.

Makes 1¼ cups.

- 1 egg
  OR: 2 egg yolks
- 1 teaspoon Dijon mustard
  OR: ½ teaspoon dry mustard
- ½ teaspoon salt
- 2 tablespoons fresh or fresh-frozen lemon juice, thawed
  OR: 1 tablespoon vinegar
- 1 cup vegetable oil
- 1 tablespoon chopped parsley

1. Break egg into container of electric blender or food processor. Add mustard, salt, lemon juice and ¼ cup of the oil; cover. Whirl on low speed.
2. With machine running, pour in remaining oil in a steady stream through removable part of lid. Stir in parsley; refrigerate.

"INSTANT" MOUSSE AU CHOCOLAT

It's just as smooth and velvety as the longer version.

Makes 8 servings.

- 1 package (6 ounces) semisweet chocolate pieces
- ⅓ cup hot brewed coffee
- 4 egg yolks
- 2 tablespoons apricot brandy or other fruit-flavored brandy
- 4 egg whites, at room temperature
- 3 tablespoons sugar

1. Combine chocolate pieces and hot coffee in the container of an electric blender; cover. Whirl at high speed for 30 seconds or until smooth.

2. Add egg yolks and brandy; cover. Whirl at high speed for 30 seconds.
3. Beat egg whites in a small bowl with an electric mixer until foamy and double in volume; beat in sugar, 1 tablespoon at a time, until meringue stands in firm peaks. Gently fold in chocolate mixture until no streaks of white remain. Spoon into 8 parfait glasses or a serving bowl.
4. Chill at least 1 hour. To serve: Garnish with whipped cream, if you wish.

FETTUCCINE IN TUNA SAUCE

Prepare the sauce while the noodles cook 15 minutes.

Makes 4 servings.

- 1 package (12 ounces) fettuccine
- ½ cup mayonnaise
- 1 can (2 ounces) flat anchovy fillets, drained
- 1 clove garlic
- 2 tablespoons lemon juice
- ½ cup cream or milk
- 1 can (7 ounces) tuna
- 2 tablespoons chopped fresh parsley
- 1 tablespoon finely slivered lemon rind
  Grated Parmesan cheese

1. Cook fettuccine in boiling salted water following label directions; drain.
2. Combine mayonnaise, anchovies, garlic, lemon juice and cream in container of electric blender; whirl until smooth. Break tuna up with a fork in a small bowl. Pour sauce over tuna.
3. Combine hot fettuccine and sauce in heated serving bowl; toss to mix well. Sprinkle parsley and lemon rind over. Serve with Parmesan cheese.

——————— •●● ———————

BLINI Russian or Polish yeast pancake, usually made with buckwheat flour. Blini, sometimes spelled *blinys*, are served in a stack, wrapped in a cloth napkin to keep them warm, and offered with a variety of toppings. They can be spread with butter or sour cream, and topped with sliced smoked fish, pickled herring, hard-cooked eggs or caviar. They are served as an appetizer when made as small silver-dollar-size pancakes.

BLINI

The perfect way to serve caviar, and well worth the time it takes.

Makes about 6 servings or 4½ dozen pancakes.

- 1 envelope active dry yeast
- 2 cups very warm milk
- 2 cups *sifted* all-purpose flour
- 1 tablespoon sugar
- 3 eggs, separated
- 3 tablespoons butter, melted
- ½ teaspoon salt
  Butter
  Dairy sour cream
  Caviar or smoked fish for topping

1. Sprinkle yeast over very warm milk in large bowl. ("Very warm milk" should feel comfortably warm when dropped on wrist.) Beat in 1½ cups of the flour and the sugar. Cover the bowl and allow the sponge to rise in a warm place about 1 hour or until double in volume.
2. Beat egg yolks, melted butter and the salt in a small bowl. Beat in the remaining flour until smooth. Beat this mixture into the sponge. Let rise again, about 30 minutes or until batter is doubled and bubbly.
3. Beat the egg whites until soft peaks form; fold into batter. Allow the batter to stand 15 minutes, then cook the blini.
4. Butter a hot large skillet and drop batter by 1½ tablespoonfuls; cook until golden brown on bottom. Turn and cook until golden on second side. Add butter to pan each time before cooking pancakes.
5. Keep blini warm, covered, in oven or chafing dish while the remaining are being cooked. Serve blini hot from chafing dish with caviar or smoked fish and sour cream or just with sour cream.

——————— •●● ———————

BLINTZ A filled and rolled pancake that is fried in butter and topped with sour cream, fruit or caviar. Possibly of Russian origin, blintzes are popular in Jewish cooking. They are usually filled with a mixture of cottage or cream cheese and egg. Enjoy them for brunch, lunch or dinner.

Blintz

CHEESE BLINTZES

We like these little packages of cheese as a dessert, although they can be served with cinnamon and sugar (instead of cherry sauce) as a main dish.

Makes 12 blintzes.

- 2 eggs
- 1¼ cups milk
- 1 cup *sifted* all-purpose flour
- ½ teaspoon salt
- 2 tablespoons butter or margarine, melted
- 2 packages (3 ounces each) cream cheese
- 1 container (12 ounces) uncreamed (dry) cottage or pot cheese
- 1 egg
- 2 tablespoons sugar
- 1 teaspoon grated lemon rind
  Butter or margarine
- 1 can (21 ounces) cherry pie filling
  Dairy sour cream

1. Beat eggs and milk just until blended in a medium-size bowl; add flour and salt; beat just until smooth. Stir in butter; chill at least 1 hour.
2. Meanwhile, beat cream cheese and cottage cheese in a small bowl until smooth. Stir in egg, sugar and lemon rind until well blended; refrigerate while preparing blintz wrappers or pancakes.
3. Heat a 7-inch skillet over medium heat. Grease lightly with butter. Pour in 3 tablespoons batter, rotating pan quickly to spread batter evenly. Cook until lightly browned on underside and dry on top. Remove from pan to a plate. Repeat with remaining batter to make 12 blintzes; stack on plate.
4. Place about 3 tablespoons filling on browned side of each blintz. Fold opposite sides over filling; then overlap ends envelope-style to cover filling completely.
5. Melt 2 tablespoons butter in a large skillet; add 5 or 6 blintzes, seamside down. Cook over low to medium heat about 5 minutes, until lightly browned on underside; carefully turn and brown other side, about 5 minutes. Keep warm in a low oven until all blintzes are browned.
6. Heat cherry pie filling in a small saucepan. Serve heated pie filling and sour cream with blintzes.

Note: To freeze blintzes, fill and fold. Place seam-side down on cookie sheet or in foil pans; cover tightly with freezer wrap. To cook, follow Step 5, cooking 10 minutes on each side or until heated through.

——————— ●●● ———————

BLUEBERRIES Blueberries are a favorite summer-time treat—eaten out of hand, served simply with cream or used in dessert, pancake and muffin recipes. The small, dark purple berries with very small seeds are the fruit of a bush found in North America, Europe and Asia. Some Americans call all blueberries "huckleberries," although huckleberries are the wild variety, found throughout New England, Virginia and Pennsylvania. In other parts of the world they are called by such names as "bilberries," "whinberries" and "whortleberries." All are varieties of blueberries.

In the United States most of the fresh blueberries are cultivated and marketed from May through August. Early supplies come from North Carolina and late crops from Michigan. An abundance is available in June, mostly from North Carolina and New Jersey. These are generally larger than the wild berries with a light blueblack color. Some people find these less flavorful.

Frozen blueberries are available year round in plastic bags.

Buying and Storing: Buy plump, firm fresh berries, uniform in size. They are sometimes covered with a waxy white bloom which is a natural protective coating. A dull appearance or soft, juicy berries indicates old berries. Blueberries have a short refrigerator life of 1 to 2 days, so use them quickly after purchasing. Freeze for longer storage.

FRESH BLUEBERRY PIE

Bake at 425° for 15 minutes, then at 350° for 35 minutes.
Makes one 9-inch pie.

- 4 cups (2 pints) fresh blueberries (or equivalent frozen, or canned, drained blueberries)
- 1 cup sugar
- ¼ cup all-purpose flour
- ¼ teaspoon salt
- 2 teaspoons grated lemon rind
- ¼ teaspoon ground cloves
- ¼ teaspoon ground cinnamon
- 1 package piecrust mix
- 3 tablespoons butter or margarine
  Milk or cream
  Sugar

1. Gently wash berries; drain well; place in a large bowl. Sprinkle with sugar, flour, salt, lemon rind, cloves, cinnamon; toss to mix. Preheat oven to 425°.
2. Prepare pastry; roll out half the pastry to a 13-inch round; fit into a 9-inch pie plate. Spoon blueberry mixture into bottom crust; dot with butter. Roll remaining pastry to a 12-inch round; cut slits in top for steam to escape. Cover pie; trim overhang to 1 inch. Pinch edges together; flute to make a stand-up edge. Brush crust with milk or cream; sprinkle with sugar. Press a collar of foil around edge of pie to prevent over-browning.
3. Bake in a preheated hot oven (425°) for 15 minutes; lower heat to moderate (350°) and bake 10 minutes; remove foil collar. Continue baking 25 minutes or until pastry is golden and juices bubble. Cool at least 1 hour on wire rack.

BLUEBERRY FOOL

Makes 6 servings.

- 2 cups (1 pint) fresh blueberries
- ¼ cup sugar
- 1½ teaspoons cornstarch
- 1 teaspoon grated lemon rind
- 1 package (3 ounces) cream cheese
- ¼ cup 10X (confectioners') sugar
- 1 teaspoon vanilla
- 1 cup heavy cream

1. Cook blueberries, sugar and cornstarch over medium heat, stirring until mixture thickens and bubbles 1 minute. Stir in lemon rind. Pour into a

5-cup glass bowl; cover and chill.

2. To serve: Beat cream cheese, 10X sugar and vanilla until smooth; add cream and beat until fluffy. Spoon mixture on top of blueberries; fold in.

BLUEBERRY MUFFINS

Bake at 425° for 20 minutes.
Makes 12 muffins.

 2 cups *sifted* all-purpose flour
 ⅓ cup sugar
 3 teaspoons baking powder
 1 teaspoon salt
 1 egg, well beaten
 1 cup milk
 ¼ cup (½ stick) butter or margarine, melted and cooled
 1 cup fresh or slightly thawed dry-pack frozen blueberries
 1 tablespoon sugar
 1 teaspoon grated lemon rind

1. Preheat oven to 425°. Sift flour, the ⅓ cup sugar, baking powder and salt into a large bowl. Mix egg, milk and melted, cooled butter in a small bowl; add all at once to flour mixture; stir lightly with a fork just until liquid is absorbed. (Batter will be lumpy.) Fold in blueberries.
2. Spoon into greased medium-size muffin-pan cups, filling each ⅔ full. Sprinkle with a mixture of the 1 tablespoon sugar and lemon rind.
3. Bake in a preheated hot oven (425°) for 20 minutes or until golden; remove from cups. Serve hot.

BLUEBERRY/STRAWBERRY-TOPPED SPONGE FLAN

Bake at 350° for 25 minutes.
Makes 12 servings.

 1 cup *sifted* all-purpose flour
 1 teaspoon baking powder
 ¼ teaspoon salt
 ⅓ cup milk
 2 tablespoons butter
 3 eggs
 1 cup sugar
 1 teaspoon vanilla
 ½ cup strawberry jelly
 1 tablespoon water
   Pastry Cream *(recipe follows)*
 7 to 8 large strawberries, hulled
 2 cups (1 pint) fresh blueberries

1. Sift flour, baking powder and salt

onto wax paper. Preheat oven to 350°.
2. Heat milk with butter just to scalding; cool slightly.
3. Beat eggs, sugar and vanilla in a medium-size bowl with electric mixer until thick and creamy. Add flour mixture alternately with milk mixture, beating after each addition. Pour into greased and floured 10-inch sponge flan pan.
4. Bake in a preheated moderate oven (350°) for 25 minutes or until top springs back when lightly pressed with fingertip.
5. Cool layer in pan on wire rack 10 minutes; loosen around edges with a knife; turn out onto wire rack; cool.
6. Heat strawberry jelly and water in a small saucepan until melted and bubbly. Brush over interior of shell and sides of cake; allow to set for 5 minutes.
7. To assemble: Fill center of sponge flan with Pastry Cream. Arrange 7 or 8 strawberries in center, stem ends down; arrange blueberries around top. Glaze berries with additional melted strawberry jelly, if desired.

PASTRY CREAM

Makes 1⅓ cups.

 1 cup milk
 4 egg yolks
 ⅓ cup sugar
 ¼ cup *sifted* all-purpose flour
 ⅛ teaspoon salt
 1 teaspoon vanilla

1. Heat milk to scalding in a medium-size saucepan.
2. Beat egg yolks with sugar in a medium-size bowl with wire whisk or electric beater until thick and creamy. Beat in flour and salt; gradually beat in scalded milk until smooth.
3. Pour mixture back into saucepan; cook, stirring constantly, until mixture thickens. (Mixture may become lumpy; if this occurs, beat with either a wire whisk or electric mixer until it becomes smooth.)
4. Lower heat and continue to cook 2 to 3 minutes, stirring constantly until mixture is very thick. Remove from heat; add vanilla; pour into small bowl. Cover with plastic wrap to keep skin from forming; chill.

BLUE CHEESE Although many countries in the world have a blue-veined cheese, Roquefort, from France, is probably the best-known variety. It is cheese made from sheep's milk, cured exclusively in the caverns of Roquefort. (Until an association of Roquefort cheese producers put an end to the practice, many kinds of blue cheese were called Roquefort.) Besides Roquefort, France produces many other blue cheeses. Some are made from cow's milk, others from a mixture of cow's, sheep's and goat's milk. French blue cheese is easily recognized by the French spelling *bleu* for the word "blue."

Italy's Gorgonzola, named after a village near Milan, is a semisoft, mildly flavored, pleasant variety of blue cheese. When it ages, it becomes sharp and crumbly in texture. Usually made from cow's milk, but sometimes blended with goat's milk, Gorgonzola forms a different type of mold than Roquefort. The Gorgonzola mold is found right in the Italian caves where the cheese is aged.

Stilton is the blue-veined cheese of England. Danish Blue or Danablu is a creamy-white, crumbly, sharp-tasting cheese originally from Denmark. The Danes also produce other blue-veined cheeses, such as Saga, which looks like a creamy Brie with the mold in the center.

The United States produces some blue cheeses: Oregon Blue from Central Point, Oregon; Treasure Cave from Faribault, Minnesota; and Maytag Blue from Newton, Iowa are the best known.

Today most of the blue-veined cheeses are no longer allowed to form mold naturally, by aging, but rather are inoculated with the mold *Penicillium roqueforti*. Although many cheeses begin with the same mold, each can take on a very different texture and taste because of a number of factors: the type of milk used, the manner by which the cheese is cured, ripened and aged. For more information, see **CHEESE**, **GORGONZOLA** and **ROQUEFORT**.

BLUE CHEESE STUFFED HAMBURGERS
Makes 4 servings.

- **2 ounces blue cheese, crumbled**
- **2 tablespoons light or heavy cream**
- **1 teaspoon grated onion**
- **1 pound ground round or chuck**
- **½ teaspoon salt**
- **⅛ teaspoon pepper**
- **1 tablespoon vegetable oil**
- **4 hamburger buns, split, toasted and buttered**

1. Combine blue cheese, cream and onion in a small bowl.
2. Tear off a 6-inch piece of wax paper. (You will have a 6 × 12-inch rectangle.) Place meat on wax paper; flatten evenly to cover the wax paper. Dip a knife in cold water, cut the meat lengthwise into two 3-inch strips, then crosswise into eight 3-inch squares.
3. Divide blue cheese mixture evenly onto 4 of the meat squares to within ¼ inch of edges. Top with the remaining squares. Lightly moisten hands with water; crimp the edges to keep the filling from seeping out during cooking. Shape into rounds. Sprinkle both sides with salt and pepper.
4. Heat oil in large skillet. Pan-fry burgers over medium heat about 5 minutes on each side or until desired doneness. (Can also be broiled or grilled 5 to 6 inches from heat, turning once.) Place between halves of hamburger buns. Garnish with cherry tomatoes, if you wish.

PARSLIED BLUE CHEESE SPREAD
This spread features a duet of two cheeses plus herbs and tangy olives.
Makes 2 cups.

- **4 ounces blue cheese, softened**
- **2 packages (3 ounces each) cream cheese, softened**
- **½ cup (1 stick) butter or margarine, softened**
- **⅓ cup chopped pimiento-stuffed green olives**
- **1½ teaspoons chopped chives**
- **¾ cup chopped fresh parsley**
- **1 small clove garlic, minced**
- **1 tablespoon brandy** *(optional)*

1. Combine blue cheese, cream cheese, butter, olives, chives, 1½ teaspoons of the parsley, garlic and brandy in a medium-size bowl; blend well.
2. Line a 2-cup bowl with plastic wrap. Turn cheese mixture into bowl, packing it down firmly; refrigerate.
3. To serve: Turn cheese ball out onto serving platter. Peel off plastic wrap. Sprinkle with remaining parsley and garnish with pimiento, if you wish.

BLUE CHEESE BUTTER
Makes ¾ cup.

- **¼ cup (½ stick) butter, softened**
- **2 ounces blue cheese, crumbled**

1. Combine butter and blue cheese in a small bowl until well mixed. Place butter mixture on wax paper and shape into a log.
2. Refrigerate until firm. Slice log. Serve cheese slices on grilled or broiled beef, chicken or veal.

——————— ●●● ———————

BLUEFISH A common sportfish caught off the Atlantic coast from Cape Cod to Florida, along the eastern coast of South America, the southern Mediterranean Sea, the Black Sea and also around Australia.

Bluefish can weigh over fifteen pounds but the smaller the fish, the milder the taste. Its flesh is oily and sometimes strong-flavored. Like tuna or mackerel, it has a fishy-tasting strip of dark meat which is usually removed.

Bluefish is highly perishable, and tastes best when fresh. Use little oil or fat in cooking. The addition of a tomato-onion sauce or a marinade of soy sauce or lemon juice enhances the flavor. Bake large fish; broil the fillets. Poaching bluefish is not recommended because the flesh is too soft. For more information, see **FISH.**

BOCKWURST Plump sausage links, pale gray in color, made from veal and pork, seasoned with a variety of herbs and spices. Bockwurst is a German specialty most often served and enjoyed with beer. To prepare, cook slowly in a frying pan until thoroughly done.

BOLOGNA American bologna bears little resemblance to the original mild sausage from Bologna, Italy. Our bologna is made from beef only or a combination of pork and beef. The meat is finely ground, seasoned, cooked and smoked. The two most familiar kinds of bologna are large sausage and ring. The large sausage is widely available presliced and sealed in transparent packages or sold in bulk and sliced to order in the delicatessen of some supermarkets.

PICKLED BOLOGNA
Makes 4 cups.

- **2½ cups water**
- **1¾ cups distilled white vinegar**
- **2 tablespoons sugar**
- **1½ teaspoons salt**
- **20 peppercorns**
- **16 whole allspice**
- **1 ring bologna (1 pound)**
- **1 large onion, sliced and separated into rings**
- **1 jar (7½ ounces) roasted peppers**

1. Combine water, vinegar, sugar, salt, peppercorns and allspice in a medium-size saucepan. Bring to boiling; lower heat; cover; simmer 10 minutes. Remove from heat; cool.
2. Slice bologna diagonally into ½-inch pieces. Layer bologna, onion rings and roasted peppers in a large glass or ceramic casserole; pour cooled pickling liquid over. Cover; chill at least 3 days before serving.

BARBECUED BOLOGNA KABOBS
Makes 4 servings.

- **1 pound unsliced bologna**
- **16 2-inch pieces green celery**
- **2 tablespoons prepared mustard**
- **2 tablespoons chili sauce**
- **2 tablespoons molasses**
- **4 cherry tomatoes**

1. Cut bologna into 1¼-inch chunks; thread with celery on 4 skewers. Place on rack over a broiler pan.
2. Combine mustard, chili sauce and molasses; brush over kabobs. Broil 5 inches from heat for 10 minutes or until glazed, turning often. To serve: Place a cherry tomato on the end of each skewer.

Pictured opposite: Bombe Glacé, page 80

Bombe

BOMBE A festive frozen dessert with a French name for the tall, cylindrical mold which originally resembled a bomb. Bombes range from very simple to very elaborate, but all have two things in common: they are made with ice cream and they are frozen in decorative molds. We've shortcut the original, more complicated version by using good quality commercial ice creams.

CHOCOLATE-RASPBERRY BOMBE

Pretty, colorful and an easy make-ahead dessert.

Makes 8 servings.

> 2 **packages ladyfingers, split**
> 1½ **pints chocolate ice cream**
> 1 **pint frozen raspberry yogurt**
> 1 **tablespoon seedless raspberry or currant jelly** *(optional)*
> **Raspberry Sauce** *(recipe follows)*

1. Line a 9×5×3-inch loaf pan with wax paper. Arrange the ladyfingers around the edges and bottom of the pan. Place in freezer to chill.
2. Soften 1 pint chocolate ice cream in a medium-size bowl in refrigerator for 30 minutes.
3. Spread the softened ice cream along the bottom and up the long side of the chilled pan with the back of a spoon to a ½-inch thickness. Return to freezer until firm.
4. Soften yogurt and remaining chocolate ice cream in separate medium-size bowls in refrigerator. Spread yogurt into center of ice cream-lined pan, leveling top. Gently spread the remaining chocolate ice cream over the entire top. Return to freezer until solid, at least 3 hours.
5. Melt jelly in a small saucepan over low heat; cool slightly. Unmold bombe; peel off wax paper. Gently brush ladyfingers with jelly. Serve with Raspberry Sauce.

RASPBERRY SAUCE

Makes about 1 cup.

> 1 **package (10 ounces) frozen raspberries, thawed**
> 1 **teaspoon cornstarch**
> 1 **tablespoon kirsch**

1. Puree raspberries in container of electric blender. Strain puree to remove seeds.
2. Blend cornstarch and puree in a saucepan; bring to boiling; lower heat; simmer 1 minute, stirring constantly, until thickened and clear.
3. Remove from heat; stir in kirsch. Refrigerate until cold.

BOMBE GLACÉ

Prepare this French ice cream dessert up to 2 months ahead.

Makes 8 to 10 servings.

> ½ **cup chopped mixed candied fruits**
> 2 **tablespoons apricot liqueur or brandy**
> 1 **quart chocolate ice cream, slightly softened**
> 1 **pint strawberry ice cream, slightly softened**
> 1 **cup heavy cream**
> ¼ **cup superfine granulated sugar**
> **Whipped cream**

1. Combine candied fruits and liqueur; let stand while preparing remainder of recipe.
2. Rinse a 6-cup fluted mold with cold water. Spread chocolate ice cream evenly around bottom and side of mold with a large spoon; freeze 30 minutes. Spread strawberry ice cream evenly over chocolate; freeze 30 minutes.
3. Beat cream in a small bowl until stiff; fold in sugar and fruits with any liqueur not absorbed. Spoon into center of mold; level off with spatula.
4. Cover mold with a piece of wax paper, then cover tightly with lid of mold or heavy-duty foil. Freeze until solid, about 3 hours.
5. Remove mold from freezer 30 minutes before serving. Run a spatula around top edge; hold a hot, wet towel around mold for 3 to 4 seconds; turn out onto chilled serving dish. Return to freezer until softened outside has refrozen.
6. Just before serving, garnish outside of bombe with whipped cream. Cut into wedges to serve.

Note: Bombe can be frosted with whipped cream and garnished with candied red cherries.

CRANBERRY-PISTACHIO BOMBE WITH PINEAPPLE GALLIANO SAUCE

Here's a festive bombe for your holiday table. It's a bit fussy to make, but worth the effort.

Makes 12 servings.

> 1 **cup water**
> 1¼ **cups sugar**
> ¾ **cup light corn syrup**
> 4 **cups fresh or frozen cranberries (16 ounces)**
> 1 **can (13 ounces) evaporated milk**
> 1 **tablespoon lemon juice**
> 2 **pints pistachio ice cream, softened**
> 2 **egg whites**
> **Pineapple Galliano Sauce** *(recipe follows)*

1. Combine water and sugar in a large saucepan. Heat until sugar is dissolved. Add corn syrup and cranberries. Cook over medium heat until cranberries pop, about 10 minutes. Cool 10 minutes.
2. Puree cranberries in container of electric blender. Add milk and lemon juice; blend well.
3. Strain mixture into a 13×9×2-inch baking pan. Cover with aluminum foil. Freeze until firm.
4. Line a 6-cup mold evenly with pistachio ice cream. Cover with aluminum foil. Freeze until firm.
5. Beat egg whites in a small bowl with an electric mixer until stiff. Turn cranberry mixture into a bowl, breaking up the lumps with a wooden spoon. Beat with same electric mixer until mixture is smooth.
6. Fold in beaten egg whites. Gently spoon mixture into lined mold. Cover with aluminum foil. Freeze until solid. To serve, unmold onto serving plate about 1 hour before serving; return to freezer to refreeze. Serve with Pineapple Galliano Sauce.

Pineapple Galliano Sauce: Combine a 20-ounce can of crushed pineapple in pineapple juice, ¾ cup sugar and 2 teaspoons cornstarch in a medium-size saucepan. Cook, stirring constantly, until sauce thickens and clears. Stir in ⅓ cup Liquore Galliano; refrigerate. Makes 3¼ cups.

BONITO A relative of the tuna (both are members of the mackerel family), bonito is found in the Atlantic and Pacific Oceans and the Mediterranean and Black Seas. Because its flesh is strong-tasting, it is not valued as the tuna and cannot, in fact, be labeled tuna in this country. Bonito is most commonly sold in cans alongside tuna, but at a lower price.

Use it in casseroles or salads where the flavor can be enhanced by other ingredients. Fresh bonito steaks are sometimes available in coastal fish markets. Dried bonito flakes are a popular ingredient in Japanese recipes.

BORDELAISE A brown sauce made with red wine and served over beef. A wine from Bordeaux, a city in the largest and finest wine region of France, is the base of this classic French sauce. The sauce was originally made by first reducing the wine with shallots, thyme, bay leaf and salt, and then adding a brown sauce and diced, poached marrow. Serve it on grilled or roasted meats; garnish with chopped parsley.

SIRLOIN OF BEEF WITH SAUCE BORDELAISE

The Bordelaise is easy to make from the pan drippings and yet so much better than ordinary gravy. And here is the serving secret: Always pour the sauce onto the plate and place the beef slices on top.

Roast at 500° for 20 minutes, then at 400° for 15 to 32 minutes.
Makes 6 servings.

3 pounds boneless sirloin, cut about 2 inches thick
  Pepper
½ cup shallots or onion, finely chopped
1 cup dry red wine
1 cup Beef Gravy *(recipe follows)*
½ teaspoon cornstarch dissolved in 1 tablespoon water
2 tablespoons butter or margarine, softened to room temperature
  Watercress

1. Sprinkle beef with pepper to taste; place on a rack in a shallow roasting pan. Preheat oven to 500°.
2. Roast in a very hot oven (500°) for 20 minutes; lower heat to hot (400°) and roast for 15 minutes more for rare. (Allow an additional 7 minutes for medium and an additional 10 minutes for well done.)
3. Remove sirloin to a heated serving platter; keep warm. Drain off all but 1 tablespoon fat from roasting pan and add the shallots, wine and Beef Gravy.
4. Bring to boiling; boil 10 minutes or until liquid is reduced by one-quarter. Lower heat; add dissolved cornstarch and stir for about 1 minute or until sauce is thickened. Add butter and mix in lightly.
5. Slice sirloin and serve on heated platter. Serve sauce separately. Garnish platter with watercress.
Beef Gravy: Cook 2 tablespoons flour and 2 tablespoons fat from roasting pan in small saucepan until browned. Gradually stir in 1 cup beef broth with a wire whisk. Cook, stirring constantly, until thickened.

— •●• —

BORSCHT There are as many recipes for this Russian and Polish soup as there are spellings—thick or thin, meat or meatless, hot or cold. Usually, but not always, borscht is made with beets, and traditionally served topped with sour cream. The most authentic recipes are made with a fermented liquid called *kvas,* brewed from rye bread, water, sugar, yeast and flour.

BORSCHT

Adding grated fresh beets to soup just before serving gives a beautiful red color. May be served hot or chilled.
Makes 6 servings.

2 carrots, pared and sliced (1 cup)
1½ cups shredded raw beets
1 turnip, pared and diced (¾ cup)
1 medium-size onion, sliced
1 cup water
2 tablespoons cider or distilled white vinegar
2 teaspoons salt

1 teaspoon sugar
6 cups Basic Beef Broth (for recipe, see BROTH)
2 cups diced boiled beef (from Basic Beef Broth)
½ small head cabbage, shredded (3 cups)
  Dairy sour cream
  Sliced rye bread

1. In a kettle combine carrots, 1 cup beets, turnip, onion, water, vinegar, salt and sugar.
2. Bring to boiling; reduce heat, cover; simmer 20 minutes. Add Beef Broth, beef and cabbage. Simmer 10 to 15 minutes longer or until all vegetables are tender.
3. Stir in remaining ½ cup beets. Ladle into soup bowls. Top with sour cream. Serve with rye bread.
For chilled soup: Refrigerate at least 4 hours before serving.
Note: Instead of Basic Beef Broth, substitute 4 cans (13¾ ounces each) beef broth and 2 cups diced roast beef.

— •●• —

BOUILLABAISSE This classic French seafood stew was created centuries ago by the fishermen on the Mediterranean coast. Each recipe differed from cook to cook, as it was simply a mixture of whatever fish were caught that day. The classic included not only fish but also eel and langoustine, a lobster-shrimp-like crustacean.

A good bouillabaisse must contain a rich fish stock, dry white wine, tomatoes and saffron. The best fish combination is of fat fish, such as mackerel, salmon or swordfish and lean fish, such as flounder, sole, halibut, cod, sea bass, snapper, sea trout or rockfish. For shellfish, use lobster, shrimp and mussels or clams. Plan to include a variety of seafood for different textures and flavors.

Traditionally the seafood is removed from the broth and served separately on a platter. The broth is then spooned over slices of French bread rubbed with garlic. More often the stew is served, fish and all, in a shallow bowl, accompanied with crusty, sliced French bread.

Bouillabaisse

CREOLE BOUILLABAISSE

This Creole version of the French classic makes good use of the bounty of the rivers, bays and Gulf waters.

Makes 8 servings.

    3 tablespoons vegetable oil
    2 tablespoons flour
    1 large onion, chopped (1 cup)
    2 cloves garlic, chopped
    1 can (28 ounces) tomatoes
 1½ teaspoons salt
    1 bay leaf
    1 teaspoon leaf thyme, crumbled
  ½ teaspoon ground allspice
  ¼ teaspoon crumbled saffron
  ¼ teaspoon cayenne
  ½ cup water
    1 cup dry white wine
    2 to 2½ pounds fish fillets (red snapper and/or bass), cut into 1½-inch pieces
  ½ pound scallops
    2 lobster tails, cut into chunks
      OR: ½ pound shelled and deveined fresh or frozen shrimp
  ½ cup sliced green onions
      French bread, sliced and toasted
      Fresh parsley *(optional)*

1. Heat oil in large Dutch oven or deep skillet; stir in flour. Cook, stirring constantly, over low to medium heat until flour turns a rich brown, about 5 minutes. Stir in onion and garlic. Cook, stirring, until soft, about 5 minutes. Add tomatoes, salt, bay leaf, thyme, allspice, saffron, cayenne and water. Bring to boiling, crushing tomatoes. Cover kettle.
2. Simmer 15 minutes; stir in wine. Add fish fillets, scallops, lobster or shrimp, and green onions; cover. Cook 5 to 10 minutes longer or just until fish is tender and flakes easily.
3. Serve in deep plates or bowls over toasted French bread. Sprinkle with chopped parsley, if you wish.
Note: Substitute with any firm white fish (halibut, cod or haddock) or substitute frozen fish cut into chunks and allow 5 to 10 minutes longer cooking time.

— ● ● ● —

BOUQUET GARNI A small herb bouquet, most often composed of fresh parsley sprigs, thyme and a bay leaf tied in cheesecloth. Dried herbs can be used in place of the fresh. Simmer the bouquet garni in stocks, stews, sauces and soups as a seasoner and remove before serving.

BOURBON An American original, this whiskey was distilled from corn by a Baptist minister in Bourbon County, Kentucky, in the 1800's and was called ''Bourbon County Whiskey.'' Bourbon must be no more than 80 proof and made from a mash containing at least 51 per cent corn. The other grains can be rye, barley or more corn. It is then aged in new charred oak barrels.

Most bourbons are labeled either Straight or Blended Straight. Straight refers to a whiskey that's full-bodied and mellow, aged two years and unblended. Blended Straight Bourbon has been blended with other Straight Bourbon. Bourbon can also be mixed with other spirits to make Blended Bourbon, which is much lighter and less expensive.

The early American colonists used bourbon as a drink, and also as a flavoring in pies, cakes and cookies.

BOURBON SWEET POTATOES

Bake at 350° for 45 minutes.
Makes 8 servings.

    4 pounds sweet potatoes or yams
  ½ cup (1 stick) butter or margarine, softened
  ½ cup bourbon
  ⅓ cup orange juice
  ¼ cup firmly packed light brown sugar
    1 teaspoon salt
  ½ teaspoon apple-pie spice
  ⅓ cup chopped pecans

1. Scrub sweet potatoes. Cook, covered, in boiling salted water to cover in a large saucepan, about 35 minutes or just until tender. Drain; cool slightly; peel the sweet potatoes.
2. Place potatoes in a large bowl; mash. Add butter, bourbon, orange juice, brown sugar, salt and apple-pie spice; beat until fluffy and smooth.
3. Spoon into a buttered 6-cup baking dish; sprinkle nuts around edge.
4. Bake in a moderate oven (350°) for 45 minutes or until lightly browned.

BOURBON STREET PECAN CAKE

Bake at 325° for 1 hour and 15 minutes.
Makes one 10-inch tube cake.

  ½ cup bourbon
    1 cup raisins
 3¼ cups *sifted* all-purpose flour
 1½ teaspoons ground nutmeg
    1 teaspoon baking powder
  ½ teaspoon baking soda
    1 cup (2 sticks) butter or margarine
 2¼ cups sugar
    5 eggs
    1 cup buttermilk
    2 cups coarsely chopped pecans
      Praline Glaze *(recipe follows)*

1. Pour bourbon over raisins; soak at least 1 hour. Sift flour, nutmeg, baking powder and baking soda onto wax paper. Grease a 10-inch tube pan.
2. Beat butter, sugar and eggs in a large bowl with electric mixer at high speed 5 minutes or until light and fluffy. Preheat oven to 325°.
3. Stir in flour mixture alternately with buttermilk, beating with a wooden spoon after each addition. Stir in raisins with any remaining bourbon and the pecans. Pour batter into prepared pan; set aside.
4. Bake in a preheated slow oven (325°) for 1 hour and 15 minutes or until center springs back when lightly touched with fingertip.
5. Cool in pan on wire rack 10 minutes; loosen cake around tube and outside edge with knife; turn out onto wire rack; cool completely. Spoon Praline Glaze over top, letting glaze dribble down the side.
Praline Glaze: Combine ½ cup firmly packed light brown sugar, ¼ cup granulated sugar and ¼ cup (½ stick) butter or margarine in small saucepan. Heat until sugar melts and mixture is bubbly; stir in ¼ cup heavy cream. Heat 1 minute; add ½ cup pecan halves and heat just until bubbly. Remove from heat; cool slightly.

Pictured opposite: Brandy Snaps, page 85

Bourbon

BOURBON BALLS

Makes 3 dozen confections.

- 1 package (6 ounces) semisweet chocolate pieces
- 3 tablespoons light corn syrup
- ¼ cup bourbon
- ½ cup sugar
- 1¼ cups crushed vanilla wafer cookies (about 36)
- 1 cup finely chopped pecans
- 1 container (4 ounces) chocolate sprinkles or jimmies

1. Melt chocolate pieces in top of a double boiler over simmering water; remove from heat. Blend in corn syrup and bourbon; stir in sugar, crushed vanilla wafers and pecans.

2. Use hands to roll mixture in balls, 1 rounded teaspoonful at a time. Roll balls in chocolate sprinkles to generously coat, pressing firmly as you roll. Place in a jelly-roll pan; cover; chill several hours.

———— •●• ————

BRACIOLE

(Also **braciola**) Pronounced *bra-CHOH-lah,* this Italian word means steak. Braciole is a braised meat roll stuffed with seasonings or vegetables, usually made with very thinly pounded round steak.

BRACIOLE

Makes 8 servings.

- 2½ pounds round steak
- ½ pound Italian sausage
- ½ cup chopped fresh parsley
- ¼ cup grated Parmesan cheese
- 1 clove garlic, minced
- 1 teaspoon Italian herb seasoning mix
- 1 teaspoon salt
- ½ teaspoon lemon-pepper seasoning
- 2 tablespoons olive oil
- 1 large onion, chopped (1 cup)
- ½ cup chopped carrot
- 1½ cups dry red wine
- 1 can (16 ounces) plum tomatoes
- 1 can (6 ounces) tomato paste
- 1 teaspoon salt
- 1 bay leaf

1. Trim all fat from steak; cut meat into 8 equal pieces; then pound until very thin with a wooden mallet.

2. Remove casing from Italian sau-sage. Break up in a medium-size bowl; add parsley, Parmesan cheese, garlic, Italian seasoning, 1 teaspoon salt and the lemon-pepper seasoning; mix thoroughly. Spread each steak with 2 heaping tablespoons of the sausage mixture; roll up, jelly-roll fashion; fasten with wooden picks or tie with string.

3. Brown beef rolls, 3 or 4 at a time, in hot oil in a Dutch oven; remove rolls and place on plate or wax paper. Add onion and carrot to pot; cook until vegetables are soft, about 5 minutes. Stir in wine, tomatoes, tomato paste, remaining 1 teaspoon salt and bay leaf; bring mixture to boiling; lower heat. Add beef rolls; cover and simmer for 1 hour. Remove from heat.

4. Remove the picks or string from braciole before serving.

———— •●• ————

BRAINS See **VARIETY MEAT.**

BRAISE A method of cooking primarily for meat, sometimes for vegetables, in which the food is browned in fat, covered and slowly cooked in a small amount of liquid. Flavorings such as onion, garlic or herbs are often added. When braising, use only enough liquid to moisten the meat.

BRAN The brown outer layer of a cereal grain, such as wheat or rye, obtained in the process of making all-purpose flour.

Bran is sold as nuggets, strips, flour or made into flakes for use as a breakfast cereal. It's a good source of carbohydrates, vitamins and minerals. Bran also provides roughage.

BRANDY Brandy is a liquid made by distilling wine, generally from grapes, then aging it. The fermented mash of other fruits — apples, peaches, pears, plums, cherries, blackberries—can also be made into a brandy but these must be labeled with the fruit name, e.g., peach brandy. Other brandies are known by special names, such as calvados which is French apple brandy; applejack is American apple brandy.

The process in making brandy first involves making wine from grapes. After that the wine is heated until it begins to evaporate and the resulting alcohol vapor passes through a condenser where it is changed into a liquid. This liquid is quite potent and so is mixed with distilled water to bring the alcohol content down to about 40 percent.

Brandies vary in aroma, taste and other characteristics according to these factors: the type of wine that it is made from, the distilling procedure and the type of wood casks that it is aged in.

The most desirable aging casks are of oak made from wood in the Limousin forests of France which imparts flavor and allows the liquid to breathe. The brandy develops an amber color and, with time, a smoothness.

A good quality brandy should age for years, that is, spend time in the wood casks. Some brandies are aged as long as 75 years. Once brandy is bottled, it ceases to age and can deteriorate in time. Those brandies that are aged longer are more expensive than those that are aged less.

Brandy is distilled in many countries, wherever wine is produced. Yet, the best brandies come from France and bear the name of the wine region from which they are distilled. For example, Cognac is a brandy from Cognac, a town in France, and only brandy made in that area can be called by that name. Armagnac is a brandy from another region in France.

Brandies of different ages are often blended. Some French brandies have initials on the labels—an indication of the style of that brandy, not of its specific age. For example, Three-Star indicates a blend of brandies with about five years of barrel aging but not less than two years. The letters V.S.O.P., which stand for Very Superior Old Pale, mean that the brandy is a blend of brandies aged longer than Three-Star, at least four years and up to ten years. Brandy is rarely labeled with the date that it was bottled since it is usually blended.

High quality brandies should be

sipped slightly warmed from a snifter (a glass that is shaped to collect the spirit's aroma). Brandy also imparts a special flavor to many meats, fruits, sauces and beverages.

BRANDIED FRUIT SAUCE

Delicious served over ice cream, plain cakes or puddings.

Makes 3½ cups.

- ½ cup golden raisins
- 1 package (6 ounces) dried apricots
- 1 cup water
- 1 can (8¼ ounces) pineapple chunks in syrup
- 1 3-inch piece stick cinnamon
- ½ cup brandy
- ¼ cup grenadine syrup
- 2 tablespoons maraschino cherries *(optional)*

1. Combine raisins and apricots with water in medium-size saucepan. Let stand 10 minutes to soften fruits.
2. Drain pineapple; add syrup to pan with cinnamon stick. Bring to boiling; lower heat; simmer 5 minutes until apricots are soft, but not mushy. Stir in brandy, grenadine, pineapple chunks and cherries. Pour into a container. Cover and store in refrigerator for at least a week. Mixture will thicken slightly on standing.

BRANDY SNAPS

Originally made as a French gaufrette (small wafer) on a hot griddle; this recipe evolved to the baked cookies below. The snaps are similar to the German hippen, which are rolled and filled with buttercream.

Bake at 300° for 10 to 15 minutes.
Makes about 4 dozen cookies.

- 1½ cups *sifted* all-purpose flour
  Pinch salt
- 2 teaspoons ground ginger
- 1 teaspoon ground nutmeg
- ¾ cup (1½ sticks) unsalted butter or margarine, melted
- 1 cup firmly packed brown sugar
- ½ cup dark molasses
- 2 tablespoons brandy

1. Preheat oven to 300°. Sift flour, salt, ginger and nutmeg into a large

bowl. Combine melted butter, sugar, molasses and brandy in a small bowl; stir into dry ingredients.
2. Drop by teaspoonfuls onto a lightly buttered cookie sheet, leaving 2½ inches between cookies.
3. Bake in a preheated slow oven (300°) for 10 to 15 minutes. Let cool only until cookies can be handled. While still warm, roll each cookie around the handle of a wooden mixing spoon to form "cigarettes." If cookies harden before being rolled, reheat in a slow oven. Cool completely; store in airtight container. Cookies can also be shaped into cones, which may be filled with a mixture of whipped cream and chopped crystallized ginger just before serving.

BRANDIED APPLE SLICES

Serve as an accompaniment to pork, ham or poultry or as a dessert.

Makes 5 cups (10 to 12 servings).

- 6 Golden Delicious apples
- 1 cup orange juice
- 2 3-inch pieces stick cinnamon
- ¾ cup sugar
- ½ cup brandy

1. Pare, halve, core and cut apples into eighths. Place in a large saucepan; add orange juice and cinnamon sticks. Bring to boiling; lower heat and simmer, covered, for 10 minutes or until apples are tender but still firm.
2. Remove from heat; stir in sugar and brandy. Cool; spoon into a container. Can be stored in refrigerator up to 1 month.

BRATWURST
A mildly seasoned pork or veal link sausage of German origin which means "frying sausage." Bratwurst is popular in many parts of Europe and also made in the United States, particularly where people of German or Scandinavian heritage live.

The meat and seasonings used to make bratwurst vary from country to country. Since it is a fresh sausage, it must be cooked thoroughly before eating. Bratwurst can be pan-fried, braised, broiled or grilled.

BRATWURST AND ONIONS IN BEER

Grill sausages 10 minutes.
Makes 4 servings (2 sausages each)

- 8 bratwursts (2 12-ounce packages)
- 3 medium-size onions, sliced
- 2 tablespoons vegetable oil
- 1 teaspoon caraway seeds, crushed
- ½ teaspoon salt
- 1 can (12 ounces) beer
- 8 frankfurter rolls or bratwurst buns, split and toasted

1. Brown bratwursts on grill close to grayed coals, about 10 minutes.
2. While sausages brown, sauté onions in oil in large saucepan on grill 2 to 3 minutes; stir in caraway seeds, salt and beer; heat to boiling. Add sausages; cover and keep saucepan on side of grill to heat at least 10 minutes. Serve on toasted frankfurter rolls or bratwurst buns.
Note: Bratwursts can be broiled or pan-fried to brown.

BRAZIL NUT
Brazil nuts are the seeds of a fruit found growing in the Amazon forest of South America. A single fruit weighing up to four pounds, produces about a dozen seeds or nuts.

The shell of each nut is difficult to crack, but once opened, a tasty nugget awaits your sampling. Brazil nuts are used in bread, cake and other dessert recipes as well as for snacks.

A high fat content is the basis of the Brazil nut's rich taste, with a single nut sporting thirty calories.

To shell Brazil nuts: Boil in water to cover about 5 minutes; drain. Let stand in cold water until cool; drain. Dry on paper toweling. Crack with a nutcracker.

To make nut curls: For garnishing cakes or pies. Boil shelled nuts in water to cover for 2 minutes. Drain and pat dry. Use a vegetable parer to make the curls. For more information, see **NUT.**

Brazil Nut Math
1 pound nuts in shells=1½ cups shelled nuts or ½ pound kernels.

Brazil Nut

BRAZIL NUT CHIPS

Bake at 350° for 12 minutes.
Makes about 2 cups.

1½ cups shelled Brazil nuts
2 tablespoons butter or
   margarine
½ teaspoon seasoned salt

1. Cover Brazil nuts with cold water in a medium-size saucepan; cover. Heat slowly to boiling; simmer 2 to 3 minutes; drain. (This softens the nuts so they can be shaved.)
2. While still warm, shave each nut lengthwise into thin slices with a vegetable parer or sharp knife. Spread in a large shallow baking pan; dot with butter.
3. Bake in a moderate oven (350°) for 12 minutes or until crisp and lightly browned, shaking pan often. Sprinkle with seasoned salt. Cool and store in a container with a tight-fitting lid.

● ● ●

BREAD The story of breadmaking parallels the history of civilization. Bread made during the Stone Age was flat or unleavened with a tough texture. It was made of crushed grains mixed with water and probably spread on stones to "bake" or dry in the sun. Later, these breads were baked in the hot ashes of a fire.

The first leavened breads were made by the Egyptians, probably by accident. One theory is that dough was left in the sun too long and began to bubble and rise because of wild yeast spores. The "soured" dough was mixed with fresh dough which upon baking produced gases that raised it to make a lighter loaf.

Excavations show that in ancient Egypt there was a community bakery in every village; a wealthy family would have its own bakery.

Breads were so highly prized that they were placed in the tombs of the dead to provide food for afterlife. Breads dating back over 3500 years have been excavated from Egyptian tombs.

The Greeks had public bakeries that produced over fifty kinds of bread. In Rome, around 100 B.C., there were over 250 bakeries. Each baker stamped the loaves he made with his own identifying mark.

In the Middle Ages, town guilds (associations of people with similar interests) formed. The bakers' guild, which actually formed during the Roman Empire, was a powerful group. Laws were enacted that protected the consumer from dishonest bakers and protected the bakers from unfair competition. The "baker's dozen" came into being during this time as bakers, in an effort to insure their business practices were beyond reproach, would add an extra loaf of bread with an order of twelve.

In Europe, the type of bread eaten was often an indication of status or wealth. During the era of William and Mary, for example, people in the rural areas ate a coarse type of barley bread or oat cakes while the upper class ate white breads made from wheat.

Bread is made of ground grain. The first grains to be used for bread were probably millet and buckwheat. Wheat and rye are the most commonly used today, but oats, barley and corn are also used. American Indians made a flat bread of maize or Indian corn long before the earliest settlers arrived. But these settlers introduced wheat to the Colonies. Breadmaking was most often done at home rather than in bakeries, unlike so much of the rest of the world.

Many countries produce breads which are special to them. For example, the French baton-like baguettes; German and Austrian black breads; Scandinavian dark breads and crisp flat breads; Irish soda bread; the British cottage loaf; Middle Eastern pita or pocket bread. Unleavened bread is eaten by Jewish people during Passover. American breads include Boston brown bread, Anadama bread (made of cornmeal and whole wheat flour) and cornbread.

Homemade breads are of two types: yeast or quick. Yeast breads, in which yeast is the leavening agent, can be either plain, savory or sweet. Quick breads, in which the leavening agent is baking soda or powder, include biscuits, loaves, muffins, doughnuts, and even pancakes.

The Making of Yeast Breads

Know Your Ingredients: *Yeast* causes dough to rise and gives bread its porous texture. Yeast is actually a small plant or cell that "grows" or multiplies under the proper temperature conditions. Yeast feeds on the sugar and produces carbon dioxide; it is this gas that causes dough to rise. It is yeast that is primarily responsible for the marvelous aromas and flavors of breads. Yeast is available as compressed cakes which must be dissolved before using or the dry granular form which can, in some recipes, be mixed directly with the dry ingredients.

Compressed yeast is moist, creamy white, and firm in texture. It is perishable and must be kept refrigerated. Look for it in the supermarket dairy case packaged in foil. It is best when used within a few days from purchase or it can be wrapped in heavy-duty aluminum foil and frozen. It keeps up to 6 months stored at 0°F. Defrost it overnight in the refrigerator before using. Compressed yeast must be dissolved in lukewarm liquid (80° to 90°) before using.

Dry yeast is a strain of yeast that has been dried and packaged in envelopes or jars. Two level teaspoons dry yeast equal a single ¼-ounce envelope or a ⅝-ounce cake. Dry yeast can be stored over 6 months unrefrigerated. In areas of the country with high temperatures, refrigeration will help keep it fresh. Dry yeast is activated by dissolving in warm liquid (110° to 115°) but can also be blended first with dry ingredients and liquid of higher temperature (120° to 130°). Dry yeast should be used before the expiration date which is stamped on the envelope.

Flour is the most essential ingredient in breadmaking. Wheat flour is the most widely used. Different varieties of wheat grain are milled and blended into flour. Wheat, especially hard wheat, is most suitable for breads because of its high gluten content. Gluten is a substance that forms an elastic network through the dough, trapping the carbon dioxide gases produced by the yeast as it feeds on and digests the sugar. Soft wheat contains less gluten and is best for quick breads, cakes and pastries. It is used primarily for cake flour.

Wheat flours are ground either from the whole kernel or from the endosperm, which is the central portion of the kernel. Flour labeled all-purpose is ground from the endosperm with the bran and germ of the kernel removed before milling. All-purpose flour is a blend of both soft and hard wheats. Most bread recipes offer a range in the amount of flour to use since the results of a recipe will be affected by the type and brand of flour to be used, the amount of moisture in the flour, the time of year it is used, and variables such as the size of eggs.

Bread flour, now currently available in some markets, is also ground from the endosperm of the wheat kernel. Similar to all-purpose flour, it has a higher gluten content than regular all-purpose flour and therefore gives excellent results in breadmaking.

Whole wheat flour is a coarse-textured flour ground from the entire wheat kernel (endosperm, bran and germ). Because whole wheat flour has a lower gluten content, baked products tend to be more dense and, therefore, heavier than those made with all-purpose flour. A lighter bread loaf is achieved when all-purpose flour is used as part of the flour in a given recipe. Stone-ground whole wheat flour is milled by coarsely crushing the wheat kernels between heavy, rotating stones. The advantages of stone grinding the wheat are that the oil in the germ is more evenly distributed and, because the grain is kept cooler during milling, rancidity is reduced. Graham flour is a whole wheat flour and can be used interchangeably in recipes calling for whole wheat flour.

Flour is also milled from other grains. Rye flour is ground from the endosperm of the rye kernel. Medium rye refers to the color of the flour. Pumpernickel rye flour is ground from the entire rye kernel and is more coarse-textured. Outside of wheat and rye, no other cereal grain contains sufficient gluten to make a satisfactory loaf of bread. Corn, bran, barley, buckwheat, soy or oats can be added to a wheat dough, but are unsatisfactory used exclusively in yeast breads.

All flour should be stored in airtight containers in the refrigerator or freezer, if possible.

Whole wheat or graham flour can be substituted for all-purpose flour in bread recipes in a ratio of 60 percent to 40 percent all-purpose flour. But the general rule when substituting flour is that the more all-purpose flour in a dough, the easier it is to knead. Whole wheat and rye breads made with whole wheat and rye flour are firmer and heavier than white breads. Rye dough requires less kneading; kneading too long increases the stickiness and makes it difficult to handle. A slightly soft, sticky dough is typical of rye flour.

Liquid, usually water or a combination of water and milk, is needed to dissolve the yeast and bind the flour. Other liquids may be used such as buttermilk, eggs, and even molasses or honey. Liquids should be at room temperature before using.

Water makes a crisp crust. Milk gives a softer crumb. Do not use milk to dissolve yeast, since the milk fat coats the yeast cells, preventing them from dissolving. (Some old-style recipes may dissolve yeast in milk.) Potato water can be used, yielding a coarser textured loaf.

Fat, added to bread dough, flavors and tenderizes the bread. Fat coats the gluten strands and shortens them to form a more tender cell structure. Fats used in bread are butter, margarine, vegetable oil or shortening. Butter or margarine are interchangeable but use only the stick form, not whipped or diet varieties. Do not substitute vegetable oil for shortening or vice versa.

Flavoring ingredients include salt, sugar, herbs, spices, raisins, nuts, berries and cheese. Although small amounts of sugar are necessary in activating the yeast, too large an amount inhibits yeast growth. Salt inhibits yeast growth so it should not be used in water in which yeast is dissolved. Raisins, nuts, berries (such as wheat berries or wheat kernels), bean or grain sprouts can be added for extra crunch just before shaping the bread loaves. If these types of flavorings are added to the dough before it has proofed the first time, the dough will be heavier, and the bread will take longer to rise.

Coarse grains like cracked wheat (the whole kernel is broken into bits) can be used to add a nutty flavor and crunchy texture. Use only a small amount of coarse grains or cook to tenderize before adding to bread dough since the sharp pieces will cut the gluten strands, resulting in a smaller loaf.

How to Mix, Knead and Shape Yeast Bread: Successful yeast baking depends on the temperature of water used to dissolve the type of yeast, the temperature at which the dough rises and the baking temperature.

When mixing the ingredients in a large bowl, use either an electric mixer or a wooden spoon. Vigorous beating causes the gluten to form more rapidly. Use only enough flour to form a soft dough that no longer clings to sides of the bowl.

Kneading is a rhythmic procedure that completes the mixing of the dough. Yeast doughs are proofed, i.e., allowed to rise and fall one or more times to improve the texture. Dough is properly proofed when double in volume. A simple test to see if the dough is proofed sufficiently is to press two fingertips lightly (½ inch) into the dough. If the dough springs back, proofing is complete. Over-proofed dough will cause the baked bread to have large holes throughout. Proofed doughs are punched down after they have risen by pushing a fist into the center of the dough to deflate it. Batter breads are not kneaded. The dough is beaten until it leaves the sides of the bowl, covered and allowed to rise.

Bread

Bake breads in a preheated oven. The final rising of the dough takes place during the first 10 to 15 minutes of baking time. When baking two loaves, place them on the center rack in the oven; for four loaves, use two racks, placed in the bottom and next to the highest positions.

Breads should be checked for doneness near the end of suggested baking time. Breads are done when nicely browned and hollow sounding when tapped lightly on top. Remove loaves from pans so they do not become soggy. Cool completely on wire racks.

The Making of Quick Breads

Quick breads are made with fast-acting leavening agents most often baking powder or soda. Air, steam and a combination of baking soda and an acid liquid, such as buttermilk or sour milk, can also cause the leavening action during baking.

Quick breads include loaves, muffins, biscuits, doughnuts, scones, shortcakes, dumplings, pancakes, waffles, popovers and spoon breads. Each differs in appearance and flavor but all are considered quick breads

How to Knead and Shape Bread

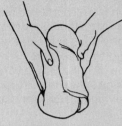

1. Turn soft dough out on floured board. Flour hands lightly, then pat dough to flatten slightly. Begin to knead this way. Pick up edge of dough with fingers and fold over toward you.

2. Push the dough away from you with the heels of both hands. If the dough sticks to the board, have a metal spatula handy to scrape the board clean; then re-flour and continue on.

3. Give dough a quarter turn, then repeat folding, pushing, turning. As you knead, you will develop your own speed. You'll find well-kneaded bread dough is satiny, elastic and smooth.

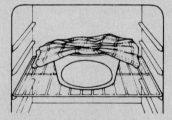

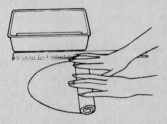

4. For an easy way to determine when dough has doubled in bulk: Press the dough flat in bowl, mark level, then remove dough. Fill bowl with water to double the first mark; mark level.

5. For warm, draft-free place to let dough rise, use oven with door closed. If the oven is electric, warm to 200°, then turn off and let cool for 5 minutes. If gas, pilot light will keep dough warm.

6. To shape a handsome loaf of bread: Roll or pat dough out to a rectangle with short side equal to length of a bread pan. Roll up the dough, in jelly-roll style, pressing the turns firmly.

7. When loaf has been shaped, make sure dough is even on both ends. Then, with fingers, pinch long seam firmly—to seal and keep from unrolling. Put in pans, with seam on bottom.

8. How to smooth ends of loaves: Press the dough down on each end of loaf with sides of hands. Tuck the thin strips formed under the loaf. Lift the loaf to the pan without stretching.

9. For shaping long loaves of bread: Roll up, in jelly-roll style, pinching seam, as in Fig. 7. Then, with the palms of your hands, taper the ends by rolling loaf back and forth on board.

because they have similar leavening action, are easy to make, fast-rising and light and porous.

Quick bread batters are of three types: soft dough, drop batters or pourable batters. Soft doughs can be rolled and shaped by hand. Biscuits, scones and doughnuts are examples of soft doughs. Examples of drop batters are muffins, cornbread, loaves and dumplings. These thick batters need only be spooned into a baking pan and take the shape of the pan utensil. Pourable batters include waffles, pancakes, Yorkshire pudding and popovers, which are made with a thin batter.

Know Your Ingredients: *Baking powder* was first made in the 1850's. Prior to that time, baked goods were leavened either by beating air into the dough or beating eggs and folding them into the dough. Another leavening agent was sourdough yeast starter. In the 1790's, a substance called pearlash was discovered which produced carbon dioxide during baking. That discovery changed breadmaking! Baking powder was another new product that worked in the same way as pearlash. Baking powder can be derived from a number of substances. A phosphate baking powder was the first type to be produced.

Another type is composed of soda and tartaric acid. The tartrate baking powders begin reacting upon being mixed with batter or dough and liquid. When using this type of baking powder, work quickly mixing the batter and bake in a preheated oven.

A third type of baking powder is a combination of ingredients which causes two rising actions instead of one as occurs in the other types of baking soda. The first rising begins in the bowl as the liquid is added. The second rising occurs when exposed to heat during baking or cooking. This double action enables you to mix the batter, yet delay baking or cooking.

All baking powders contain baking soda and an acid and are activated when mixed with a liquid. The chemical reaction produces carbon dioxide bubbles, which, when heat is applied, cause the dough to expand and the heat sets the dough at this point.

Baking soda (bicarbonate of soda) works only when combined with an acid substance (such as in baking powder mixtures) or when an acidic liquid—buttermilk, sour milk, chocolate, honey, corn syrup or molasses—is used.

Some recipes use both baking powder and baking soda. The baking soda neutralizes an acidic ingredient while the baking powder provides the leavening action.

Flour forms the framework of quick breads. All-purpose flour is most often used. Flour with a low gluten content is desirable for making quick breads.

Fats such as shortening, vegetable oil, butter or margarine are used to add flavor, richness, tenderness and moisture to quick breads. Use the type of fat specified in the recipe.

Liquid ingredients bind the dry ingredients. Milk, buttermilk, sour cream or yogurt add moisture to the bread.

Eggs add flavor, a golden color, and tenderness to bread. Unless otherwise specified, recipes calling for eggs refer to eggs graded large.

Flavoring ingredients include sugar, which gives dough tenderness, flavor and aids in browning. Herbs, spices, bacon bits, nuts, shredded vegetables, mashed bananas, chocolate, raisins or grated peel are frequently added to quick breads helping to give each bread its distinct flavor.

How to Mix Quick Breads:

Biscuit method: Soft dough quick breads are made using the following method. First the dry ingredients are stirred together. The fat is then cut into the dry ingredients with a pastry blender or two knives until the mixture resembles coarse crumbs. Today's food processors make quick work of this. Liquid is added and stirred lightly just to make a soft dough. The dough is then gently kneaded 8 to 10 *times* (not minutes). The kneaded dough is ready to be cut or shaped.

Muffin method: Drop batters are made using the following method. The dry ingredients are stirred together and in a separate bowl, the liquid ingredients are stirred together. The liquid ingredients are gradually added to the dry ingredients and mixed just until the dry ingredients are moistened. Overmixing will result in peaked muffins with large holes inside.

The Effects of High Altitudes

High altitudes, i.e., over 5,000 feet, cause breads to rise faster and higher. If a recipe calls for two envelopes or cakes of yeast, use only one. Watch the proofing closely. Punch dough down and bake, even if not yet double in volume as long as finger indentation remains in dough. In quick breads, the amount of baking powder and baking soda needs to be decreased also. For best results, use recipes designed for high altitudes.

Hints for Better Breads

• Use the specified pan size called for in the recipe. A pan that is too large will yield a flat bread. Too small a pan will cause the dough to overflow.

• The material the pan is made of can affect the baking time. Uncoated metal pans need longer baking. Glass and enamel pans need a lower oven temperature. Reduce the oven temperature called for in the recipe by 25 degrees.

• For shiny crust on a loaf of yeast bread, brush it with an egg beaten with a little water. For a soft crust, rub with softened butter or margarine just after the bread is removed from the pan to cool.

Storing Bread

Completely cooled yeast breads, when properly wrapped in freezer paper, heavy foil or heavy plastic bags, can be frozen for up to 6 months. If bread is to be used for sandwiches, slice it before freezing. The frozen slices will pull apart easily and thaw quickly.

Quick breads are better if allowed to stand overnight. When completely cool, wrap in foil or plastic wrap and store at room temperature.

Yeast Breads These are traditional or everyday yeast breads. For sweet yeast breads, see **COFFEE CAKE, ROLL.**

SESAME POTATO TWIST LOAF

Bake at 400° for 10 minutes, then at 350° for 35 minutes.
Makes 2 loaves.

½ cup (1 stick) butter or margarine
½ cup sieved hot cooked
   potatoes or prepared instant
   potatoes
2 tablespoons sugar
2 teaspoons salt
1 cup milk, scalded
2 envelopes active dry yeast
⅓ cup very warm water
5½ cups all-purpose flour
1 egg white slightly beaten with
   1 tablespoon water
   Sesame seeds

1. Combine butter and potatoes in a large bowl; stir until melted. Add sugar, salt and milk; stir until mixture is smooth. Cool to lukewarm.
2. Dissolve yeast in very warm water("very warm water" should feel comfortably warm when dropped on wrist); stir into potato mixture. Stir in 3 cups of the flour, beating with a spoon until smooth. Gradually stir in enough of the remaining flour to make a moderately firm dough which does not stick to sides of bowl. Turn out on a lightly floured board and knead until smooth and elastic, about 10 minutes, working in only as much additional flour as needed (about 1 cup) to prevent dough from sticking.
3. Place dough in a large buttered bowl; turn dough to bring buttered side up. Cover and let rise in a warm draft-free place until double in bulk, about 50 minutes.
4. Punch dough down and turn out onto lightly floured surface. Divide into four parts. Roll each part between buttered palms to form a strand about 15 inches long. Spiral-wrap two strands to form a twisted loaf; tuck ends under. Place in a buttered 9 × 5 × 3-inch loaf pan. Repeat with remaining strands. Cover and let rise in a warm place until almost double in bulk, about 20 to 30 minutes.

5. Preheat oven to 400°. Gently brush tops of loaves with egg white mixture; sprinkle on sesame seeds.
6. Bake in a preheated hot oven (400°) for 10 minutes. Lower heat to moderate (350°) and bake for 35 minutes or until golden brown. Turn loaves out to cool on wire racks.

HONEY WHEAT BREAD

Bake at 400° for 15 minutes, then at 350° for 30 minutes.
Makes 3 medium-size loaves.

2 envelopes active dry yeast
4 cups very warm water
3 tablespoons honey
1 tablespoon vegetable oil
2 teaspoons salt
5 cups unbleached all-purpose flour
5 cups whole wheat flour

1. Sprinkle yeast over very warm water in a large bowl ("very warm water" should feel comfortably warm when dropped on wrist); stir to dissolve. Stir in honey and oil. Let stand 10 minutes, until bubbly.
2. Stir in salt, 1 cup white flour and 1 cup whole wheat flour; stir well. Continue adding flour until 8 cups have been incorporated. Turn out onto lightly floured surface. Knead in enough of the remaining flour to make a smooth ball. Knead 10 minutes, until smooth and elastic.
3. Place in large greased bowl, turning to bring greased side up. Let it rise 45 minutes to an hour in a warm place away from drafts. Punch down. Divide into 3 parts.
4. Pat out each part to make a 12 × 8-inch rectangle; roll up from short end; place in greased 8 × 4 × 3-inch pans. Cut slashes 1-inch deep on tops of loaves. Preheat oven to 400°. Let loaves rise in warm place about 10 minutes.
5. Bake in a preheated hot oven (400°) for 15 minutes. Lower heat to moderate (350°) and bake 30 minutes longer or until bread sounds hollow when tapped. Remove from pans to wire racks to cool completely.

GRANOLA-YOGURT LOAVES

Bake at 375° for 35 to 40 minutes.
Makes 2 round loaves.

2 envelopes active dry yeast
1½ cups very warm water
1 teaspoon honey
1 container (8 ounces) plain yogurt
3 teaspoons salt
5 to 5½ cups *sifted* unbleached all-purpose flour
2 cups natural cereal with fruits and nuts
1 egg white slightly beaten with 1 tablespoon water

1. Sprinkle yeast into ½ cup of the very warm water in a 1-cup measure; stir in honey. ("Very warm water" should feel comfortably warm when dropped on wrist.) Stir until yeast dissolves. Let stand, undisturbed, to proof until bubbly and double in volume, about 10 minutes.
2. Combine remaining water, yogurt and salt in large bowl; stir in yeast mixture. Beat in 4 cups of the flour with electric mixer at medium speed for 2 minutes. Stir in cereal. Gradually stir in remaining flour to make a stiff dough.
3. Turn out onto lightly floured surface; knead until smooth and elastic using only enough flour to keep dough from sticking, about 10 minutes.
4. Place in buttered large bowl; turn to bring buttered side up. Cover with a towel or wax paper. Let rise in a warm place, away from draft, 1 hour or until double in bulk.
5. Punch dough down; turn out onto lightly floured board; knead a few times; invert bowl over dough; allow to rest 10 minutes. Divide dough in half and knead each half a few times; shape into two round loaves. Place on a large greased cookie sheet, 5 inches apart.
6. Let rise in a warm place, away from draft, 40 minutes or until double in bulk. Preheat oven to 375°. Cut a ½-inch deep cross in the top of each with a sharp knife. Brush with beaten egg white.
7. Bake in preheated moderate oven (375°) for 35 minutes or until golden brown and loaves sound hollow when tapped. Remove from cookie sheet to wire racks; cool completely.

Pictured opposite, counterclockwise, from upper left: Cinnamon Nut Coffee Ring, page 94; Georgian Cheese Bread, page 93; Golden Orange Rolls, page 93; Lemon Cheese Braid, page 93; Cheese Puffs, page 94; Meat Piroshki, page 93

Bread

OLD-FASHIONED RYE BREAD

Bake at 400° for 35 minutes.
Makes 2 loaves.

- 2 envelopes active dry yeast
- 2½ cups very warm water
- ¼ cup light molasses
- 4 teaspoons salt
- 2 tablespoons vegetable shortening
- 2½ cups rye flour
- 1 tablespoon caraway seeds, crushed
- 5½ to 6 cups *sifted* all-purpose flour
  Cornmeal

1. Sprinkle yeast into ½ cup of the very warm water; stir in 1 teaspoon of the molasses. ("Very warm water" should feel comfortably warm when dropped on wrist.) Stir until yeast dissolves. Let stand to proof, undisturbed, until bubbly and double in volume, about 10 minutes.
2. Combine remaining water and molasses with salt and shortening in a large bowl; stir in yeast mixture, rye flour and caraway seeds; add enough all-purpose flour to make a soft dough.
3. Turn out onto lightly floured surface. Knead until smooth and elastic, about 10 minutes, using enough of the remaining flour to keep dough from sticking.
4. Place in buttered large bowl; turn dough to bring buttered side up. Cover with towel. Let rise in a warm, draft-free place, 1 hour or until double in bulk.
5. Butter a large cookie sheet. Sprinkle lightly with cornmeal.
6. Punch dough down; turn out onto lightly floured surface; knead 3 to 4 times; invert bowl over dough; let rest 10 minutes. Divide dough in half and knead each half 3 to 4 times. Shape into 2 loaves. Place loaves at least 4 inches apart on prepared cookie sheet.
7. Let rise again in a warm place, away from draft, 45 minutes or until double in bulk. Preheat oven to 400°. Brush tops with water.
8. Bake in a preheated hot oven (400°) for 35 minutes or until browned and loaves sound hollow when tapped. Remove from cookie sheet to wire rack; cool completely.

Easy Yeast Breads

If you love warm, fresh bread, but don't have time to knead and wait for the dough to rise twice, try these easy mix-and-bake breads. The electric mixer does much of the work for you. The results are delicious—their flavor and fragrance may have you baking your own bread regularly.

ALFALFA WHEAT BREAD

A nutty, moist casserole bread that's nutritious and easy to prepare.

Bake at 375° for 30 to 35 minutes.
Makes 1 round loaf.

- 1 cup water
- ½ cup plain yogurt
- 2 tablespoons molasses
- 1 cup *unsifted* all-purpose flour
- 1 envelope active dry yeast
- 2 teaspoons salt
- 1½ to 2 cups *unsifted* whole wheat flour
- 1 cup alfalfa sprouts, coarsely chopped
  Cornmeal

1. Heat water, yogurt and molasses in a small saucepan over low heat just until very warm, about 120°. (Mixture will appear curdled.)
2. Combine flour, yeast and salt in a large bowl. Gradually beat in yogurt mixture with electric mixer on low speed until mixed. Beat in 1½ cups whole wheat flour slowly. Beat batter on medium speed 2 minutes; increase speed to medium-high; beat 2 minutes more.
3 With spoon, stir in sprouts and enough of the remaining whole wheat flour to make a soft dough that will stay in a mound. Cover bowl with a towel. Let rise in a warm place, away from draft, until double in volume, about 45 minutes.
4. Grease a 1½-quart casserole dish; sprinkle bottom and side with cornmeal or packaged bread crumbs. Stir dough and turn into prepared dish. Sprinkle top with more alfalfa sprouts, if you wish. Cover with towel. Let rise in a warm place, away from draft, until almost double in volume, 45 minutes.
5. Bake in a moderate oven (375°) for 30 minutes or until golden brown and bread sounds hollow when lightly tapped with fingertips.
6. Loosen bread around edge with metal spatula; remove to wire rack; cool completely. Wrap in foil or plastic; store in refrigerator.

PUMPERNICKEL RAISIN BREAD

Bake at 375° for 40 minutes.
Makes 1 loaf.

- 2 packages active dry yeast
- 1 cup whole wheat flour
- 1 cup rye flour
- 1½ cups *sifted* all-purpose flour
- ½ cup instant dry milk powder
- 2 teaspoons salt
- 1½ cups very warm water
- ¼ cup molasses
- 2 tablespoons vegetable oil
- ½ cup raisins

1. Mix yeast, whole wheat flour, rye flour, ½ cup of the all-purpose flour, dry milk and salt in a large bowl.
2. Add water, molasses and oil ("very warm water" should feel comfortably warm when dropped on wrist); beat with electric mixer at medium speed, 3 minutes. Stir in remaining flour to make a stiff dough. Stir in raisins.
3. Cover bowl with a towel. Let dough rise in a warm place, away from drafts, 45 minutes or until double in volume.
4. Stir dough down. Spoon into greased 9×5×3-inch loaf pan, pushing dough well into corners.
5. Let rise again in a warm draft-free place, 35 minutes or until double in volume. Preheat oven to 375°.
6. Bake in a preheated hot oven (375°) for 40 minutes or until bread sounds hollow when tapped. Cool on wire rack.

Frozen Bread Dough

Bread dough, commercially frozen and ready for you to thaw and use, is a miracle worker. It can be turned into all kinds of wonderful breads and coffee cakes. You can buy plain, frozen bread dough or sweet dough.

GOLDEN ORANGE ROLLS

Bake at 350° for 25 minutes.
Makes 16 rolls.

- **1 loaf (14 ounces) frozen sweet dough, thawed**
  OR: 1 loaf plain dough, thawed overnight in refrigerator
- **⅓ cup firmly packed brown sugar**
- **2 tablespoons butter, softened**
- **1 orange**
- **¼ cup slivered almonds**
- **¼ cup granulated sugar**
- **⅓ cup golden raisins**

1. Allow dough to stand at room temperature on a lightly floured surface for 1 hour. Roll and push dough to a 20×9-inch rectangle. Let rest while making filling.
2. Combine brown sugar and butter in small bowl. Grate rind from orange (1 tablespoon) and reserve. Squeeze juice from orange; stir 2 tablespoons into brown sugar mixture. Spread in bottom of 9×9×2-inch baking pan. Sprinkle with almonds.
3. Mix orange rind and granulated sugar. Stir in raisins; sprinkle over dough.
4. Roll jelly-roll fashion from long side. Cut into 1¼-inch slices. Place in prepared pan; cover with cloth and let rise 45 minutes, until double in volume. Preheat oven to 350°.
5. Bake in a preheated moderate oven (350°) for 25 minutes. Invert onto serving platter. Serve warm.

GEORGIAN CHEESE BREAD

Bake at 375° for 35 minutes.
Makes 8 servings.

- **1 loaf (1 pound) frozen plain bread dough, thawed overnight in refrigerator**
- **16 ounces Muenster cheese**
- **2 eggs**
- **½ teaspoon salt**
- **½ cup dairy sour cream**
- **1 tablespoon butter or margarine**

1. Allow dough to stand at room temperature on a lightly floured surface for 1 hour. Roll dough into 9-inch circle. Continue to roll and pat dough to make larger circle 18 to 20 inches in diameter. Let rest while making the cheese filling.
2. Shred Muenster cheese into large bowl. Beat eggs in small bowl; measure out 2 tablespoons; reserve; stir remaining eggs, the salt and sour cream into cheese in bowl, mixing thoroughly.
3. Generously butter a 9-inch pie plate. Place dough loosely in pan, draping excess over sides. Spoon in filling, making a flat circle. Gather the dough loosely to the center of the filling, turning pan as you go, pleating the folds. Twist ends into a topknot in center of the pie. Let rest 30 minutes. Preheat oven to 375°. Brush top of dough with reserved egg.
4. Bake in a preheated moderate oven (375°) for 35 minutes. If crust is browning too fast, lower temperature to 350°. Let cool slightly and cut into wedges.

LEMON CHEESE BRAID

Bake at 350° for 30 minutes.
Makes 1 braid.

- **1 loaf (14 ounces) frozen sweet dough, thawed overnight in refrigerator**
  OR: 1 loaf (1 pound) frozen plain dough, thawed overnight in refrigerator
- **1 package (8 ounces) cream cheese, softened**
- **1 egg yolk**
- **2 tablespoons sugar**
- **½ teaspoon vanilla**
- **1 teaspoon grated lemon rind**
- **1 egg, beaten with 1 teaspoon water**

1. Allow dough to stand at room temperature on a lightly floured surface for 1 hour. Roll and push to a 16×8-inch rectangle. Let rest while making filling.
2. Beat cheese, egg yolk, sugar and vanilla in small bowl with electric mixer. Stir in lemon rind.
3. Place dough on large greased cookie sheet; spread cheese down center third of dough. Cut dough from outside to filling, spacing cuts 1 inch apart. Overlap dough strips alternately from left and right to cover cheese mixture.
4. Brush braid with egg mixture; let stand in warm place 30 minutes. Preheat oven to 350°.
5. Bake in a preheated moderate oven (350°) for 30 minutes. Remove to rack. Serve warm.

MEAT PIROSHKI

Bake at 400° for 30 minutes.
Makes 6 servings.

- **1 loaf (1 pound) frozen plain bread dough, thawed overnight in refrigerator**
- **1 large onion, chopped (1 cup)**
- **2 tablespoons butter or margarine**
- **1 pound lean ground round or chuck**
- **4 hard-cooked eggs, finely chopped**
- **1 teaspoon dried dillweed**
  OR: 1 tablespoon fresh dill, snipped
- **1 teaspoon salt**
- **¼ teaspoon pepper**
- **¼ cup dairy sour cream**
- **1 egg yolk, beaten with 1 teaspoon water**

1. Allow dough to stand at room temperature on a lightly floured surface for 1 hour. Roll ⅔ of the dough to a 12-inch circle and remaining ⅓ to a 9-inch circle. Let dough rest; prepare filling.
2. Sauté onions in butter in large skillet until soft, about 5 minutes. Stir in meat, cooking until pink color is gone.
3. Add eggs, dillweed, salt, pepper and sour cream to meat mixture. Let cool slightly.
4. Line a greased 9-inch pie plate with the 12-inch circle of dough. Spoon in filling, mounding slightly in center; brush edge of dough with egg mixture. Top with remaining dough circle. Gently fold edge toward center, firmly pressing edges together. Decorate with scraps of dough. Let rise for 30 minutes. Preheat oven to 400°. Brush again with egg.
5. Bake in a preheated hot oven (400°) for 30 minutes. If dough is browning too fast, lower temperature to 375° and cover top with foil.
6. Remove to wire rack to cool slightly; serve warm.

Bread

CHEESE PUFFS

Bake at 400° for 12 minutes.
Makes about 6 dozen.

> 1 loaf (1 pound) frozen plain
> bread dough, thawed overnight
> in refrigerator
> 2½ ounces Swiss cheese,
> shredded (⅔ cup)
> ½ teaspoon salt
> ⅛ teaspoon cayenne
> ½ cup grated Parmesan and
> Romano cheeses
> 1 egg yolk, beaten with 1
> teaspoon water

1. Allow dough to stand at room temperature on a lightly floured surface 1 hour. Roll and pat out to ½ inch thick. Sprinkle with Swiss cheese, salt and cayenne. Fold dough over to enclose cheese. Knead into a ball.
2. Sprinkle surface with all but 1 tablespoon mixed cheeses; continue to knead until dough has incorporated all the cheese.
3. Roll out to a 12-inch square. Cut into 1½-inch squares or use 1½-inch round cutter. Re-roll trim. Place on greased cookie sheets. Let rise 30 minutes.
4. Preheat oven to 400°. Brush cheese puffs with egg yolk mixture, then top each with a pinch of reserved cheese.
5. Bake in a preheated hot oven (400°) for 12 minutes. Remove to wire rack to cool slightly; serve warm.

CINNAMON-NUT COFFEE RING

Bake at 350° for 25 minutes.
Makes 1 coffee cake.

> 1 loaf (14 ounces) frozen sweet
> dough, thawed overnight in
> refrigerator
> OR: 1 loaf (1 pound) frozen
> plain dough, thawed overnight
> in refrigerator
> ½ cup (1 stick) butter, softened
> ½ cup chopped walnuts
> ½ cup sugar
> 2 teaspoons ground cinnamon
> Confectioners' Glaze (recipe
> follows)

1. Allow dough to stand at room temperature on a lightly floured surface for 1 hour. Roll and push dough to a 14 × 8-inch rectangle.
2. Spread ⅔ of the dough with all but 2 tablespoons of the butter; fold entire rectangle in thirds. Tap gently with rolling pin. Turn dough so open edge faces you and roll out again. Fold in thirds again. Let rest 15 minutes while making filling.
3. Combine nuts, sugar and cinnamon in small bowl. Roll dough to 14 × 8-inch rectangle. Spread remaining 2 tablespoons butter over surface; sprinkle with cinnamon-sugar mixture almost to edges. Roll jelly-roll fashion from long side. Place seam-side down on greased jelly-roll pan and shape into a circle, pinching seam well to seal.
4. Using scissors, make deep cuts from outside almost to center, 1 inch apart. Turn each section cut-side up so filling shows. Cover; let rise until double in volume, about 1 hour. Preheat oven to 350°.
5. Bake in a preheated moderate oven (350°) for 25 minutes. Remove to wire rack. Cool. Drizzle with Confectioners' Glaze.

Confectioners' Glaze: Blend ½ cup 10X (confectioners') sugar with 1 tablespoon milk in a small bowl.

Quick Breads It's easy to see why quick breads are always a favorite. You can make a loaf of bread in very little time, with no kneading or waiting for the dough to rise. For other quick breads, see **BISCUIT, DOUGHNUT, DUMPLING, MUFFIN, PANCAKE, POPOVER, WAFFLE, YORKSHIRE PUDDING.**

CARROT-WALNUT BREAD

Bake at 350° for 1 hour.
Makes 1 loaf.

> 1 cup vegetable oil
> ¾ cup sugar
> 2 eggs
> 1 teaspoon vanilla
> 1½ cups sifted all-purpose flour
> 1½ teaspoons baking soda
> 1½ teaspoons ground cinnamon
> ½ teaspoon salt
> 3 large carrots, grated (1½ cups)
> 1½ cups ground walnuts
> Lemon Glaze (recipe follows)

1. Preheat oven to 350°. Grease and flour a 9 × 5 × 3-inch loaf pan.
2. Combine vegetable oil, sugar, eggs and vanilla in a large bowl.
3. Sift flour, baking soda, cinnamon and salt onto wax paper; add to sugar mixture; stir in carrots and walnuts; mix until just blended. Turn into prepared pan.
4. Bake in a preheated moderate oven (350°) for 1 hour or until center springs back when lightly pressed with fingertip. Cool bread in pan 10 minutes. Turn out onto wire rack; cool completely. Spread top with Lemon Glaze.

Lemon Glaze: Combine ½ cup 10X (confectioners') sugar, 1 teaspoon grated lemon rind and 1 tablespoon lemon juice in a small bowl; stir until smooth; drizzle over top and sides of Carrot-Walnut Bread.

ORANGE WHOLE-WHEAT BREAD

Bake at 350° for 1 hour.
Makes 1 loaf.

> 2 cups sifted all-purpose flour
> 1 cup sugar
> 3½ teaspoons baking powder
> 1 teaspoon salt
> 1 cup whole wheat flour
> ¾ cup crunchy nut-like cereal
> nuggets
> 1 egg
> 4 teaspoons grated orange rind
> ¾ cup orange juice
> ¾ cup milk
> ¼ cup (½ stick) butter, melted

1. Sift all-purpose flour, sugar, baking powder and salt into a large bowl. Stir in whole wheat flour and cereal nuggets. Preheat oven to 350°.
2. Beat egg slightly in small bowl. Stir in orange rind and juice, milk and butter.
3. Pour liquid ingredients into dry and stir just until flour is evenly moist. Spoon batter into greased 9 × 5 × 3-inch loaf pan.
4. Bake in a preheated moderate oven (350°) for 1 hour or until a wooden pick inserted in the center comes out clean. Cool in pan on wire rack 10 minutes. Remove from pan; cool completely. Wrap in foil or plastic when cool; store overnight.

STEAMED GINGER BROWN BREAD

Makes 2 loaves.

- **1 package gingerbread mix**
- **¼ cup yellow cornmeal**
- **1 teaspoon salt**
- **1½ cups milk**
- **1 cup raisins**

1. Combine gingerbread mix, cornmeal and salt in a large bowl; stir in milk until mixture is evenly moist; beat at medium speed with electric mixer 2 minutes, or 300 vigorous strokes by hand; stir in raisins.
2. Pour batter into 2 greased 1-pound coffee cans; cover with foil; fasten with string to hold tightly.
3. Place cans on a rack or trivet in a kettle or steamer (or make a rack by crumpling foil in a doughnut shape to fit bottom of kettle); pour in boiling water to half the depth of cans; cover.
4. Steam 3 hours or until bread is firm and a long skewer inserted in center comes out clean. (Keep water boiling gently during entire cooking time, adding more boiling water, if needed.)
5. Cool bread in cans on a wire rack 5 minutes. Loosen around edges with a knife; turn out onto rack; cool. Slice and serve warm or cold.

BRIDIE'S IRISH SODA BREAD

Bake at 400° for 40 minutes.
Makes 1 loaf.

- **4 cups *sifted* all-purpose flour**
- **1 tablespoon sugar**
- **1½ teaspoons salt**
- **1 teaspoon baking soda**
- **1 cup dried currants**
- **1½ cups buttermilk**

1. Preheat oven to 400°. Sift flour, sugar, salt and baking soda into a large bowl; stir in currants to coat with flour.
2. Stir in buttermilk, just until flour is moistened. Knead dough 10 times in bowl with lightly-floured hands.
3. Turn dough out onto lightly floured cookie sheet and shape into an 8-inch round. Cut a cross into the top with a floured knife.
4. Bake in a preheated hot oven (400°) for 40 minutes or until loaf turns golden and sounds hollow when tapped. Cool completely on wire rack before slicing.

COUNTRY CORN BREAD

Bake at 450° for 25 minutes.
Makes two 8 × 8 × 2-inch breads.

- **1½ cups yellow cornmeal**
- **2 cups *sifted* all-purpose flour**
- **2 tablespoons sugar**
- **4 teaspoons baking powder**
- **1 teaspoon salt**
- **2 eggs**
- **2 cups milk**
- **¼ cup bacon drippings or shortening, melted**

1. Preheat oven to 450°. Combine cornmeal, flour, sugar, baking powder and salt in a large bowl. Add eggs and milk. Stir to make a smooth batter; stir in bacon drippings.
2. Pour into 2 greased 8 × 8 × 2-inch baking pans.
3. Bake in a preheated very hot oven (450°) for 25 minutes or until crusty and golden brown. Cool slightly in pans on wire racks; serve warm.

CHEDDAR POPPY STRIPS

Bake at 425° for 10 minutes.
Makes 16 strips.

- **2 cups buttermilk baking mix**
- **½ teaspoon leaf basil, crumbled**
- **½ cup milk**
- **2 tablespoons butter or margarine, melted**
- **1 package (4 ounces) shredded Cheddar cheese (1 cup)**
- **1 teaspoon poppy seeds**

1. Preheat oven to 425°. Place baking mix and basil in a large bowl. Stir in milk with fork until a soft dough forms.
2. Knead dough 3 to 4 times on a floured board. Roll out into a 16 × 10-inch rectangle; brush with 1 tablespoon of the melted butter; sprinkle cheese evenly over dough.
3. Fold in thirds lengthwise. You will have a 16 × 3-inch strip.
4. Brush with remaining butter; sprinkle with poppy seeds; cut crosswise into 16 1-inch strips. Place on ungreased cookie sheet.
5. Bake in a preheated hot oven (425°) for 10 minutes or until strips are golden brown. Serve warm.

SPOON BREAD

Bake at 350° for 40 minutes.
Makes 4 to 6 servings.

- **5 eggs**
- **4 teaspoons baking powder**
- **¼ cup white cornmeal**
- **1 tablespoon sugar**
- **½ teaspoon salt**
- **2 cups milk**
- **2 tablespoons butter or margarine, melted**

1. Preheat oven to 350°. Beat eggs with baking powder until foamy in a medium-size bowl.
2. Stir in cornmeal, sugar, salt, milk and melted butter. Pour into a greased 6-cup baking dish.
3. Bake in a preheated moderate oven (350°) for 40 minutes or until puffed and golden. Serve hot in place of potatoes or bread.

DEVILED HAM AND CHEESE PINWHEELS

Bake at 450° for 10 minutes.
Makes 16 pinwheels.

- **1 can (2¼ ounces) deviled ham**
- **2 ounces Swiss cheese, shredded (½ cup)**
- **2 tablespoons butter, melted**
- **1 teaspoon freeze-dried chives**
- **2 packages (7.5 ounces each) refrigerated buttermilk biscuits**

1. Preheat oven to 450°. Combine ham, cheese, butter and chives in a small bowl; reserve.
2. On a lightly floured board, place 4 biscuits in a horizontal row overlapping each halfway; place 4 more biscuits in a row below and overlapping the first row. Continue with remaining biscuits to form an 8-inch square.
3. Roll out with lightly floured rolling pin into 10 × 16-inch rectangle. Press together any open spaces.
4. Spread ham and cheese filling evenly over dough.
5. Roll up jelly-roll fashion from long side, keeping roll 16 inches long. Cut into 1-inch pieces with scissors. Tuck end of roll underneath pinwheel and place on buttered cookie sheet.
6. Bake in a preheated very hot oven (450°) for 10 minutes or until lightly browned. Serve warm with butter.

Bread

ONION ROUNDS

Bake at 400° for 15 minutes.
Makes 10 rolls.

- ⅓ cup instant minced onion
- ⅓ cup water
- 1 package (7.5 ounces) refrigerated buttermilk or country-style biscuits (10 biscuits)
- 1 egg

1. Combine onion and water in a bowl. Let stand 10 minutes. Preheat oven to 400°.
2. Flatten each biscuit into a 3-inch round with a rolling pin; place on lightly buttered cookie sheet.
3. Beat egg in small bowl. Brush on each roll with a pastry brush.
4. Drain water from onion; blot onion between paper toweling; sprinkle evenly over all rolls.
5. Bake in a preheated hot oven (400°) for 15 minutes or until golden brown. Serve warm.

— ● ● ● —

BREAD LEFTOVER Ready-made leftover bread can be put to many other uses. So, don't throw that heel away! It can be cubed for a stuffing or bread pudding, added to soup or gravy as a thickener, made into bread crumbs or cubes for croutons. Bread can also be used to make "stratas," an inexpensive baked egg custard main dish.

To Make Cubes and Croutons

Soft Bread Cubes Stack 2 or 3 slices of bread on a cutting board and cut into strips of desired width; then cut across the strips to form even-size cubes. Trim crusts off bread slices before cutting into cubes, if you wish.

Toasted Bread Cubes Spread soft bread cubes in a jelly-roll pan and place in a slow oven (300°). Toast, shaking occasionally, until golden brown on all sides.

Croutons Brown soft bread cubes, about 1 cup at a time, in 2 tablespoons olive or vegetable oil in a large, heavy skillet over moderately high heat, stirring and turning often until evenly golden brown.

Garlic Croutons Sauté 1 clove garlic, crushed, in 2 tablespoons olive or vegetable oil in a large skillet over moderate heat until golden. Discard the garlic. Add 1 cup soft bread cubes to garlic-flavored oil. Sauté, stirring and turning often until cubes are evenly golden brown. Drain on paper toweling.

To Make Bread Crumbs

Fresh Bread Crumbs Tear slices of bread into small pieces with your fingers. Or, place one slice at a time, quartered, in the container of an electric blender or food processor; cover; whirl at high speed 15 seconds.

Dry Bread Crumbs Put dry bread slices through a food chopper fitted with a fine blade. (A neat trick is to tie a plastic bag on the blade end of the grinder so that the crumbs will drop directly into the bag as they are ground—no mess.) Or, place slices of dry bread in a plastic bag and seal; crush with a rolling pin. Or, fastest trick of all, whirl dry bread pieces in the container of an electric blender or food processor.

For fine crumbs: Sift the ground crumbs through a fine sieve. Store the fine crumbs and the coarse (those left behind in the sieve) separately in covered containers.

Buttered Bread Crumbs Melt 2 tablespoons butter or margarine in a skillet; add 1 cup of dry bread crumbs and stir-fry until crumbs are golden brown. Makes 1 cup.

Seasoned Bread Crumbs Prepare Buttered Bread Crumbs and remove from heat. Stir in 2 tablespoons chopped fresh parsley, 2 tablespoons grated Parmesan cheese, ½ teaspoon leaf basil, crumbled, ½ teaspoon leaf oregano, crumbled and dash of pepper.

Bread Math

½ cup soft bread cubes = 1 (⅝-inch) slice soft bread
⅓ cup dry bread cubes = 1 (⅝-inch) slice dry bread
⅓ cup toasted bread cubes = 1 (⅝-inch) slice soft bread
½ cup fresh bread crumbs = 1 (⅝-inch) slice soft bread
¼ cup dry bread crumbs = 1 (⅝-inch) slice dry bread

CHILI PIE CASSEROLE

Bake at 375° for 45 minutes.
Makes 8 servings.

- Cornbread (*recipe follows*)
- ¾ pound ground chuck
- 1 medium-size onion, chopped
- 2 teaspoons salt
- 1 tablespoon plus 1 teaspoon chili powder
- 1 can (6 ounces) tomato paste
- 2 cups water
- 4 ounces Cheddar cheese, shredded (1 cup)
- 4 eggs, slightly beaten
- 3 cups milk

1. Make Cornbread. Remove cooled cornbread from pan; carefully split cooled cornbread crosswise to make 2 thin layers. Cut bottom layer into nine 2½-inch squares. Cut each square to make 2 triangles. Crumble remaining layer and place in bottom of well buttered 11¾ × 7½ × 1¾-inch baking pan.
2. Sauté meat and onion in heavy skillet 5 minutes. Stir in 1 teaspoon of the salt, the chili powder, tomato paste and water. Cook, uncovered, stirring occasionally, 15 minutes. Spread over cornbread in pan. Sprinkle with ½ cup of the cheese.
3. Arrange cornbread triangles on top. Combine eggs with milk and remaining teaspoon of salt. Pour over cornbread. Sprinkle with remaining ½ cup cheese. Cover and chill at least 1 hour or overnight.
4. Bake uncovered in a moderate oven (375°) for 45 minutes or until puffed and golden. Remove to wire rack. Let stand 10 minutes before serving.

Note: Cover tips of cornbread with foil if they are browning too rapidly.

Cornbread: Preheat oven to 425°. Combine 1 cup cornmeal, 1 cup *sifted* all-purpose flour, 4 teaspoons baking powder and ½ teaspoon salt in a large bowl. Stir in 1 cup milk, 1 egg and ¼ cup vegetable shortening. Beat until fairly smooth, 1 minute. Pour into greased 8 × 8 × 2-inch pan. Bake in a preheated hot oven (425°) for 20 minutes or until top springs back when lightly touched with fingertip; cool in pan on wire rack.

Pictured opposite: Clockwise from upper right: Spinach Cheese Strata, page 98; Chili Pie Casserole, page 96; Curried Egg Strata, page 98

Bread Leftover

FREEZER ORANGE FRENCH TOAST

Bake at 500° for 13 to 18 minutes.
Makes 4 to 6 servings.

- 4 eggs
- 1 cup milk
- 2 tablespoons sugar
- 1 teaspoon vanilla
- 1 teaspoon grated orange rind
- ¼ cup orange juice
- ¼ teaspoon freshly ground nutmeg
- 8 to 10 slices day-old French bread, ¾ inch thick
  Butter or margarine, melted
  10X (confectioners') sugar

1. Beat eggs, milk, sugar, vanilla, orange rind and juice and nutmeg. Place bread on a jelly-roll pan. Pour egg mixture over bread and let stand a few minutes; turn slices over and let stand until all egg mixture is absorbed. Place in freezer, uncovered, until firm; transfer to freezer bag and return to freezer.
2. To serve: Preheat oven to 500°. Place frozen slices on greased jelly-roll pan. Brush each with melted butter or margarine.
3. Bake in a preheated very hot oven (500°) for 8 minutes. Turn slices, brush again and bake 5 to 10 minutes longer or until lightly browned. Serve with confectioners' sugar, honey or maple syrup, if you wish.

CURRIED EGG STRATA

For a pleasant flavor combination, serve with chutney or pickled melon rind.

Bake at 375° for 45 minutes.
Makes 4 servings.

- ¼ cup mayonnaise
- 1 teaspoon curry powder
- 4 slices firm whole wheat bread, lightly toasted
- 4 slices firm white bread, lightly toasted
- 3 hard-cooked eggs
- ¼ cup chopped green onions
- 2 ounces Swiss cheese, shredded (½ cup)
- 3 eggs
- 2½ cups milk
- 1 teaspoon salt

1. Combine mayonnaise and curry powder in small bowl. Spread on two slices of the whole wheat and two slices of the white bread. Cut slices into quarters. Place in bottom of buttered 6-cup shallow baking pan.
2. Slice hard-cooked eggs and place on top of bread. Sprinkle with green onions and the cheese.
3. Cut remaining 4 slices bread into quarters. Arrange in checkerboard design over the cheese.
4. Beat eggs slightly in medium-size bowl; stir in milk and salt. Pour over bread slices.
5. Cover and chill at least 1 hour or overnight.
6. Bake uncovered in a moderate oven (375°) for 45 minutes or until puffed and golden. Remove to wire rack. Let stand 10 minutes before serving.

APPLE-BREAD PUDDING

Bake at 350° for 40 minutes.
Makes 6 servings.

- ¼ cup dried currants or raisins
- 2 tablespoons apple cider or juice
- 1 large tart cooking apple (Rome Beauty or Granny Smith)
- ¼ cup (½ stick) butter or margarine, melted
- 4 eggs, beaten
- 1¾ cups milk
- ½ cup heavy cream
- ½ cup sugar
- ½ teaspoon vanilla
- 2 cups *unseasoned* croutons
- ⅓ cup slivered almonds
- 2 tablespoons brown sugar

1. Soak currants in the apple cider while preparing other ingredients.
2. Peel, core and cut apple into very thin slices. Cook slices in 2 tablespoons of butter in a small skillet just until soft and translucent; spoon into a 1½-quart casserole.
3. Beat eggs in a medium-size bowl. Add milk, cream, sugar and vanilla and stir to blend well.
4. Add croutons, remaining butter and currant mixture to casserole; stir gently to mix with apples.
5. Pour custard mixture into casserole and let stand 20 minutes until croutons are soaked with custard.

Sprinkle with almonds and sugar.
6. Place casserole in a large, shallow baking pan; place on oven shelf. Pour boiling water into pan to come 1 to 2 inches up sides of casserole.
7. Bake in a moderate oven (350°) for 40 minutes or until a thin-bladed knife comes out clean when inserted 1 inch from edge. Serve warm or cold with heavy cream, if you wish.

SPINACH CHEESE STRATA

The flavor of this convenient dish is similar to a spinach quiche.

Bake at 375° for 45 minutes.
Makes 6 servings.

- 1 loaf French bread (day-old is best)
- 1 large onion, chopped (1 cup)
- 2 tablespoons butter
- ¾ cup cooked, chopped spinach (8 cups fresh)
  OR: 1 package (10 ounces) frozen chopped spinach, thawed
- 1 teaspoon dillweed
- 1 teaspoon salt
  Pinch pepper
- 6 ounces Swiss cheese, shredded (1½ cups)
- 3 eggs
- 2½ cups milk

1. Cut bread into thin slices; line bottom of buttered shallow 6-cup baking dish with half the slices.
2. Sauté onion in butter in large skillet 5 minutes. Squeeze spinach dry and add to pan with dill, ¼ teaspoon of the salt and the pepper. Stir just to combine.
3. Spread spinach over bread in pan; sprinkle with 1 cup of the cheese. Arrange remaining bread overlapping on top.
4. Beat eggs in medium-size bowl; stir in milk and remaining ¾ teaspoon salt. Pour over bread. Sprinkle with remaining cheese. Cover and chill at least 1 hour or overnight.
5. Bake uncovered in a moderate oven (375°) for 45 minutes or until puffed and golden. If bread is browning too quickly, cover with foil. Remove to wire rack. Let stand 10 minutes before serving.

●●●

BRICK CHEESE An American original, brick cheese is a firm, rectangular-shaped, strong-flavored cheese. It was first made by a dairyman of Swiss ancestry in Dodge County, Wisconsin around the 1850's. He had drained the cooked curd of his cheese into a brick-shaped mold and put bricks on top to press the curd and separate the whey. The resulting cheese was golden-yellow with tiny holes and a pungent odor. It slices easily and is a delicious addition to grilled sandwiches. For more information, see **CHEESE**.

BRIE This popular French cheese is named for the province east of Paris where it is produced. It is now made in the United States. Considered the cheese of kings because so many French monarchs preferred it, Brie is a creamy white, soft cheese which is mild-flavored and becomes pungent upon ripening. It is made in round, flat molds; a wheel of Brie ranges from 7 to 22 inches in diameter. It has a grayish-white edible crust. Skimmed cow's milk (sometimes with added cream) is used to make this cheese. Serve Brie at room temperature for an appetizer or with fruit as dessert. For more information, see **CHEESE**.

FRIED BRIE

Makes 12 servings

- 1 **small Brie cheese (7-inch wheel)**
  Flour
- 1 **egg**
- 1 **tablespoon water**
- ½ **cup packaged bread crumbs**
- 2 **tablespoons butter**
- 1 **loaf French bread**

1. Remove and discard paper and plastic wrapping from cheese. Coat all surfaces with flour.
2. Beat egg with water in a pie plate until foamy. Dip cheese in egg, then in crumbs, coating well.
3. Heat butter in a small skillet or flame-proof casserole just until it foams. Place Brie in skillet; cover; cook over low heat about 5 minutes or until golden brown on one side.

Turn and cook, covered, on other side until golden brown.
4. Remove from heat; make a cut in the cheese, so it will run. Serve at once with the bread which has been cut in small pieces. Pass around to guests while warm. (Cheese will become firm as it cools.)

Note: Brie may be prepared through Step 2, covered and refrigerated for 1 day before serving.

● ● ●

BRIOCHE A yeast bread of French origin, brioche is usually served as a bun or roll with morning coffee. It can be hollowed and filled with a creamy meat or fish mixture. Brioche is characterized by a small round ball of dough on top. It has a rich, brown crust, golden interior and a buttery flavor. Brioche can be baked in different shapes, but is typically baked in one large or several individual fluted brioche pans. The first brioche might have been made in Brie, hence the name.

BRITTLE A type of candy that is so hard it must be broken into small pieces for serving. Brittle is generally made with sugar, syrup and nuts which are boiled to a very high temperature and then poured onto a surface to cool and harden. See also **CANDY**.

ALMOND BRITTLE

Makes about ¾ pound.

- 1 **cup sugar**
- ½ **cup light corn syrup**
- ½ **cup water**
- ¼ **teaspoon salt**
- 1 **tablespoon butter or margarine**
- 1 **cup whole unblanched almonds or peanuts**
- 1 **teaspoon baking soda**

1. Butter a large cookie sheet.
2. Combine sugar, corn syrup, water, salt and butter in a large saucepan. Cook, stirring constantly, until sugar dissolves. Cover pan for 1 minute to allow the steam to wash down the sugar crystals that cling to side of pan, or wipe down the crystals with a damp cloth.
3. Uncover pan; insert candy ther-

mometer. Cook, without stirring, until candy thermometer reaches 270° (soft crack stage, where syrup, when dropped into very cold water, separates into hard, but not brittle, threads).
4. Remove from heat; stir in almonds; return to heat. Continue cooking until candy thermometer reaches 300° (hard crack stage, where syrup, when dropped into very cold water, separates into threads that are hard and brittle).
5. Remove from heat; stir in baking soda. Let foaming syrup settle slightly, then quickly pour onto prepared cookie sheet and stretch out as thinly as possible with the aid of 2 forks. Cool completely, then break in pieces. Store up to 3 weeks in tightly-covered containers, separating the layers with foil or plastic wrap.

GINGER SESAME BRITTLE

Makes 1½ pounds.

- 1½ **cups sesame seeds (about 3 jars, 2¾ ounces each)**
- 1 **cup sugar**
- 1 **cup dark corn syrup**
- ¼ **cup water**
- 2 **tablespoons butter or margarine**
- 1 **teaspoon baking soda**
- ¼ **cup finely chopped crystallized ginger**

1. Toast sesame seeds in a skillet over moderate heat, stirring occasionally.
2. Butter a jelly-roll pan or other rimmed baking sheet.
3. Combine sugar, corn syrup, water and butter in a large saucepan. Bring to boiling, stirring constantly. Lower heat and cook, without stirring, until mixture reaches 300° on a candy thermometer or until a small amount of syrup, when dropped into very cold water, separates into threads that are hard and brittle.
4. Remove from heat; stir in sesame seeds, baking soda and ginger. Pour into prepared pan, spreading quickly with spatula to fill pan. Cool, then break into pieces. Store in tightly-covered containers with foil or plastic wrap between layers.

Brittle

PEANUT BRITTLE

Makes 2¾ pounds.

- **3 cups sugar**
- **1¼ cups water**
- **½ cup light corn syrup**
- **3 tablespoons butter or margarine**
- **1 pound Spanish peanuts**
- **1 teaspoon baking soda**
- **1 tablespoon water**
- **1½ teaspoons vanilla**

1. Butter 2 large cookie sheets.
2. Combine sugar, water and corn syrup in a large, heavy saucepan. Bring to boiling over medium heat, stirring constantly.
3. Boil mixture, without stirring, until candy thermometer registers 270° (soft crack stage). Remove from heat. Add butter and peanuts.
4. Continue cooking until candy thermometer registers 300°. (A teaspoonful of syrup will separate into brittle threads when dropped in cold water.) Remove from heat. Mix baking soda with the 1 tablespoon water; add to hot candy with vanilla.
5. When bubbles subside, pour candy onto the prepared cookie sheets as thinly as possible. Cool; break into pieces. Store in airtight container with wax paper between the layers.

— ●●● —

BROCCOLI A member of the *Brassica* family of vegetables, along with cauliflower, Brussels sprouts, cabbage, kale and kohlrabi, broccoli is the unopened flower buds that grow on thick stalks. It is believed to have originated in Italy; the name is derived from *brocce,* meaning a branch or shoot.

Broccoli can be traced as far back as 2,000 years ago to the Romans and Greeks. Italian immigrants first planted this vegetable in America, but it wasn't until the 1920's that it was commercially grown.

This dark green vegetable is a good source of vitamins A and C. A serving of 3½ ounces or 100 grams is only 28 calories.

Buying and Storing: There are many fresh varieties of broccoli available in autumn, winter and spring. Some are dark green, others purplish-green. It is also sold frozen as spears or chopped for year-round use.

Choose fresh broccoli with tight, firm buds, no yellow flowers, and stalks that are not cracked or woody. Bunches can vary in size; a 2-pound bunch makes about 4 servings. Store broccoli in plastic bags in the refrigerator crisper.

To Prepare: Wash broccoli when ready to use. Cut a thin slice from the bottom of each stem or stalk. Discard outer leaves. Split the stalks lengthwise into ½-inch-thick pieces. With a small knife, peel off the outer layer, beginning at the bottom and peeling to the base of the flowerets. If the spears are too long, cut them in half crosswise. For stir-frying, cut them into 2-inch lengths.

To Cook: Place spears in a saucepan with about ½ inch of boiling water. Cover and cook until just tender, about 10 minutes. Drain and serve, seasoned with butter, salt and pepper.

To Stir-Fry: Heat oil in a large skillet or wok. Cut broccoli into small pieces. Add to skillet and stir-fry 1 minute. Add a small amount of soy sauce or water. Cover and cook 2 to 3 minutes. Season with salt.

To Microwave: In a 13 × 9-inch dish, pour ½ cup water. Arrange 1 to 1½ pounds fresh broccoli spears in dish so that the flowerets are in the center. Cover with vented plastic wrap; microwave on high power 4 minutes. Rotate dish. Microwave 4 more minutes. Let stand 2 minutes. Drain and season with butter, salt, pepper or seasoned bread crumbs.

BROCCOLI SAUTÉ

Makes 6 servings.

- **1 bunch fresh broccoli (about 2 pounds)**
- **3 tablespoons peanut or vegetable oil**
- **2 cups chopped celery**
- **3 tablespoons soy sauce**
- **½ teaspoon ground ginger**

1. Trim outer leaves and tough ends from broccoli; cut stems and flowerets crosswise into ½-inch-thick slices. (There should be about 6 cups.) Wash; drain.
2. Heat oil in a large skillet; stir in broccoli and celery. Cook, stirring constantly, 4 minutes, or just until wilted. Stir in soy sauce and ginger; cover skillet.
3. Steam 10 to 12 minutes or until vegetables are crisp-tender.

BROCCOLI AND HAM SOUFFLÉ

Bake at 350° for 35 minutes.
Makes 4 servings.

- **2 tablespoons chopped onion**
- **3 tablespoons butter or margarine**
- **3 tablespoons flour**
- **½ teaspoon salt**
- **⅛ teaspoon pepper**
- **1 cup milk**
- **4 eggs, separated**
- **1 package (10 ounces) frozen chopped broccoli, thawed**
- **1 cup finely chopped cooked ham (about 4 ounces)**
- **3 tablespoons grated Parmesan cheese**
- **1 teaspoon cream of tartar**

1. Sauté onion in butter in a medium-size saucepan, stirring occasionally, until tender but not brown, about 2 minutes. Stir in flour, salt and pepper; cook 1 minute. Stir in milk until mixture is smooth. Cook, stirring constantly, until mixture thickens.
2. Beat egg yolks slightly in a small bowl; stir in a little of the hot mixture; return blended mixture to saucepan. Cook over low heat, stirring constantly, 2 minutes. Preheat oven to 350°.
3. Drain broccoli in a colander, pressing with a spoon to remove excess moisture. Stir into sauce along with ham and cheese. Remove from heat.
4. Beat egg whites with cream of tartar in a large bowl until soft peaks form. Gently fold broccoli mixture into whites until no streaks of white remain. Spoon into a lightly greased 1½-quart soufflé or other straight-sided dish.
5. Bake in a preheated moderate oven (350°) for 35 minutes or until browned and puffed and a knife inserted 1 inch from edge comes out clean. Serve at once.

CREAM OF BROCCOLI SOUP

Makes 6 servings.

- **1 bunch fresh broccoli (about 1½ pounds)**
- **1 medium-size onion, chopped (½ cup)**
- **2 tablespoons butter or margarine**
- **1 potato, pared and diced (1 cup)**
- **2 cans (13¾ ounces each) chicken broth**
- **½ teaspoon salt**
  Dash cayenne
- **1 cup light cream or half-and-half**
- **⅛ teaspoon ground nutmeg**

1. Trim outer leaves and tough ends from broccoli. Separate stalks and cut into 2 or 3 shorter lengths. Parboil in boiling salted water in a large saucepan 5 minutes; drain well.
2. Sauté onion in butter in a large saucepan for 5 minutes, until soft but not brown. Add potato, chicken broth, salt and cayenne. Heat to boiling; lower heat; simmer 15 minutes. Add broccoli, reserving a few flowerets for garnish; simmer 5 minutes longer or until vegetables are tender.
3. Pour mixture, half at a time, into the container of electric blender; cover; whirl until smooth. Return mixture to saucepan; add cream and nutmeg; bring to boiling (if soup is too thick, add more cream or milk). Taste and add more salt, if needed. Garnish with reserved flowerets.

BROCCOLI CUSTARD RING

Bake at 350° for 30 minutes.
Makes 8 servings.

- **1 large bunch broccoli (about 2½ pounds)**
- **4 eggs, beaten**
- **1½ teaspoons salt**
- **¼ cup heavy cream**
- **¼ teaspoon pepper**
- **¼ teaspoon ground nutmeg**
- **2 teaspoons butter, softened**

1. Cook broccoli in boiling salted water in a large kettle or Dutch oven, about 10 minutes or until tender. Drain; cool. Chop into small pieces to fit an electric blender or food processor; cover; blend until pureed.
2. Combine the broccoli puree, eggs, salt, heavy cream, pepper and nutmeg in a large bowl. Butter a 4-cup ring mold with the softened butter. Spoon the broccoli mixture into the mold and cover with foil.
Note: If made ahead, refrigerate at this point.
3. Place mold in larger pan; pour in boiling water to a 1-inch depth.
4. Bake in a moderate oven (350°) for 30 minutes or until custard is set. Unmold onto warm serving dish.

PASTA WITH BROCCOLI

Makes 8 servings.

- **1 bunch fresh broccoli (about 2 pounds)**
  OR: 1 package (10 ounces) frozen broccoli spears
- **2 tablespoons olive or vegetable oil**
- **2 large cloves garlic, halved**
- **1 pepperoni sausage (about 8 ounces), diced (about 1½ cups)**
- **1 package (1 pound) bow-tie noodles**
- **¼ cup (½ stick) butter or margarine**
- **1 cup grated Parmesan cheese**

1. Trim fresh broccoli, removing leaves and cutting a thin slice from the bottom of each stem. Cut broccoli stems into julienne pieces, leaving the flowerets whole. Wash broccoli flowerets and stems.
2. Cook fresh broccoli stems in lightly salted boiling water in a large skillet 5 minutes; add flowerets and cook 5 minutes longer or until broccoli is crisp-tender; drain well. Or, cook frozen broccoli following label directions; drain well.
3. Heat oil in same skillet with garlic pieces for 5 minutes, but do not allow the garlic to brown. (This gives garlic a bitter taste.) Remove garlic pieces with a slotted spoon; add diced pepperoni and cook about 5 minutes. Add broccoli and brown lightly.
4. Cook pasta, following label directions; drain and return to kettle. Add butter and toss to coat evenly. Add Parmesan cheese and toss well; then add broccoli-pepperoni mixture and toss gently to distribute evenly in pasta.
5. Turn out onto heated serving platter and serve with additional Parmesan cheese, if you wish.

———————— •●● ————————

BROIL This method of cooking was probably used as early as mankind discovered fire. Broil means to cook on a grill or under direct heat. It is both fast and a calorie-saver, since there generally is no need to use additional fat.

BROTH A clear meat, fish, poultry or vegetable stock or a combination made from these ingredients. Broth is often used interchangeably with stock and bouillon. A broth can be frozen, but be sure to leave adequate space in the container to allow for expansion. Keep some on hand to make soups and sauces, to moisten stuffings, and to cook rice or vegetables.

Basic beef and chicken broths are wonderfully delicious by themselves, but they are also the start of some equally fabulous variations. Make them on a day you have a little time. Let them bubble leisurely until their rich broth has captured all the goodness from the meat and vegetables. You may want to use some right away; if not, just pack them away in the freezer.

TURKEY BROTH

Makes 8 cups.

- **Carcass of 12- to 14-pound turkey**
- **2 quarts water**
- **2 celery stalks, broken in half**
- **1 carrot, pared and quartered**
- **1 onion, quartered**
- **6 peppercorns**
- **1 large bay leaf**
- **1 tablespoon salt**

1. Combine all ingredients in large kettle. Bring to boiling; lower heat to simmer. Cook uncovered 2 to 3 hours. Strain through colander.
2. When bones are cool enough to handle, remove meat and use in recipes. Chill broth in refrigerator. Remove fat from surface of broth.

Broth

CREAM OF TURKEY SOUP

Makes 6 servings.

- 1 teaspoon salt
- ⅛ teaspoon pepper
- 5 cups Turkey Broth (recipe on page 101) or Basic Chicken Broth (recipe below)
- 1 large carrot, pared and chopped
- ½ cup chopped celery
- 2 medium-size leeks, washed well and chopped (1 cup)
- 1 small parsnip, pared and chopped (½ cup)
- 1 tablespoon dry sherry (optional)
- ½ cup light cream
- 1 cup chopped cooked turkey
- 2 tablespoons chopped parsley or watercress

1. Add salt and pepper to broth in a large saucepan; heat to boil. Add carrot, celery, leeks and parsnip. Lower heat; simmer until vegetables are barely soft, about 20 minutes. Remove from heat.

2. Pour soup through strainer into bowl. Puree vegetables in electric blender. Return puree and broth to pan. Add sherry, cream and turkey to soup.

4. Heat just to simmering over medium heat. Do not boil. Add parsley; serve.

BASIC CHICKEN BROTH

It is well worthwhile to make home-made chicken broth. This recipe gives you enough broth and meat to make 2 soups and even extra meat for a salad or casserole, if you wish.

Makes 12 cups.

- 2 broiler-fryers (3 to 3½ pounds each) Chicken giblets
- 2 medium-size carrots, pared
- 1 large parsnip, pared
- 1 large onion, chopped (1 cup)
- 2 celery stalks
- 2 celery tops
- 3 sprigs parsley
- 1 leek, washed well Water
- 2 tablespoons salt
- 12 peppercorns

1. Combine chicken, chicken giblets, carrots, parsnip, onion and celery in a large kettle; tie celery tops, parsley and leek together with a string; add to kettle. Add enough cold water to cover chicken and vegetables, about 12 cups.

2. Heat slowly to boiling; skim; add salt and peppercorns; reduce heat. Simmer very slowly for 1 to 1½ hours or until chicken is very tender. Remove meat and vegetables from broth, discard the bundle of greens.

3. Strain broth through cheesecloth into a large bowl. (There should be about 12 cups.) Use this delicious broth in the following soup recipe or in any of our recipes calling for chicken broth.

4. When cool enough to handle, remove and discard skin and bones from chicken; cut meat into bite-size pieces; use as called for in following recipe, or use in salads, casseroles, etc. To store in refrigerator up to 3 or 4 days, keep in covered container. To freeze, pack in small portions (1 or 2 cups) in plastic bags or freezer containers, to use as needed.

5. To store in refrigerator up to 4 days, leave fat layer on surface of broth until ready to use, then lift fat off and discard, or use in other cooking. To freeze, transfer broth to freezer containers, allowing space on top for expansion. Freeze until ready to use (3 to 4 months maximum).

MULLIGATAWNY SOUP

This classic soup has its origins in India and is richly flavored with exotic curry.

Makes 6 servings.

- 3 medium-size carrots, pared and sliced
- 2 celery stalks, sliced
- 6 cups Basic Chicken Broth (see above)
- 3 cups diced cooked chicken (from Basic Chicken Broth)
- 1 large onion, chopped (1 cup)
- ¼ cup (½ stick) butter or margarine
- 1 apple, pared, quartered, cored and chopped
- 5 teaspoons curry powder
- 1 teaspoon salt
- ¼ cup all-purpose flour
- 1 tablespoon lemon juice
- 2 cups hot cooked rice
- ¼ cup chopped fresh parsley
- 6 lemon slices (optional)

1. Cook carrots and celery in 1 cup Chicken Broth in a medium-size saucepan 20 minutes or until tender. Add chicken; heat just until hot; cover; keep warm.

2. Sauté onion until soft in butter or margarine in Dutch oven; stir in apple, curry powder and salt; sauté 5 minutes longer or until apple is soft; add flour. Gradually stir in remaining chicken broth; heat to boiling, stirring constantly; reduce heat; cover; simmer 15 minutes.

3. Add vegetables and chicken with the broth they were cooked in; bring just to boiling. Stir in lemon juice.

4. Ladle into soup plates or bowls; pass hot cooked rice and chopped parsley and lemon slices, if you wish, as a garnish.

BASIC BEEF BROTH

This flavorful beef broth is the basic stock for a variety of soups to follow.

Makes 14 cups.

- 2½ pounds brisket, boneless chuck, or bottom round, in 1 piece
- 2 pounds shin of beef with bones
- 2 3-inch marrow bones
- 1 veal knuckle (about 1 pound) Water
- 8 teaspoons salt
- 2 carrots, pared
- 2 medium-size yellow onions, peeled
- 2 celery stalks with leaves
- 1 turnip, pared and quartered
- 1 leek, washed well
- 3 large sprigs parsley
- 12 peppercorns
- 3 whole cloves
- 1 bay leaf

1. Place beef, shin of beef, marrow bones and veal knuckle in a large kettle; add water to cover, about 4 quarts. Heat to boiling; skim off foam that appears on top. Add salt, carrots, onions, celery, turnip and leek; tie parsley, peppercorns, cloves and bay

Brownies

leaf in a small cheesecloth bag; add to kettle. Push under the liquid and add more water, if needed.

2. Heat to boiling; cover; reduce heat; simmer very slowly 3½ to 4 hours or until meat is tender. Remove meat and vegetables from broth.

3. Strain broth through cheesecloth into a large bowl. (There should be about 14 cups.) Use this broth in the following soup recipe or in any of our recipes calling for beef broth.

4. When meat is cool enough to handle, remove and discard bones. Trim large piece of meat and save for other recipes, if you wish. Cut trimmings and shin beef into bite-size pieces; use as called for in following recipe. To store in refrigerator up to 3 to 4 days, keep in covered container. To freeze, pack in small portions (1 or 2 cups) in plastic bags or freezer containers, to use as needed.

5. To store in refrigerator up to 4 days, leave fat layer on surface of broth until ready to use, then lift off and discard before heating. To freeze, transfer broth to freezer containers, allowing space on top for expansion. Freeze until ready to use (3 to 4 months maximum).

OLD-FASHIONED BEEF AND VEGETABLE SOUP

Makes 8 servings

1½ quarts Basic Beef Broth (recipe on page 102)
 2 potatoes, peeled and diced (2 cups)
 2 carrots, pared and sliced
 1 cup sliced celery
 2 small onions, peeled and quartered
 1 can (16 ounces) tomatoes
 2 teaspoons salt
 ⅛ teaspoon pepper
 ½ head green cabbage, shredded (2 cups)
 1 cup frozen whole-kernel corn
 3 cups diced boiled beef (from Basic Beef Broth)
 1 tablespoon chopped parsley

1. Heat Beef Broth to boiling in a large saucepan or kettle; add potatoes, carrots, celery, onions, tomatoes, salt and pepper; heat to boiling

again; reduce heat; cover; simmer 20 minutes.

2. Stir in cabbage, corn and meat; simmer 10 minutes longer or just until all vegetables are crisp-tender. Sprinkle with parsley.

3. Ladle into soup bowls.

——————— ●●● ———————

BROWNIES Children love them and so do adults. A truly American concoction, according to legend, the first brownies were a fallen chocolate cake. Whatever their beginnings, these bar cookies are favorites for snacks, picnics and lunchboxes.

DELUXE ORANGE-FROSTED BROWNIES

Bake at 350° for 30 minutes.
Makes about 36 squares.

 ¾ cup *sifted* all-purpose flour
 ¼ teaspoon baking soda
 ¼ teaspoon salt
 ½ cup sugar
 ⅓ cup vegetable shortening
 2 tablespoons water
 1 package (6 ounces) semisweet chocolate pieces
 1 teaspoon vanilla
 2 eggs
1½ cups coarsely chopped walnuts
 ¼ cup golden rum or orange juice
 Orange Frosting (recipe follows)
 Chocolate Icing (recipe follows)

1. Sift flour, baking soda and salt onto wax paper. Preheat oven to 350°.
2. Combine sugar, shortening and water in a medium-size saucepan. Heat, stirring constantly, until sugar melts and mixture comes to boiling. Remove from heat; stir in chocolate pieces and vanilla until smooth.
3. Beat in eggs, 1 at a time. Stir in flour mixture and walnuts. Spread evenly in a greased 9 × 9 × 2-inch pan.
4. Bake in a preheated moderate oven (350°) for 30 minutes or until shiny and firm on top. Remove from oven; sprinkle rum over top; cool completely.
5. Spread Orange Frosting smoothly over top; chill until firm. Spread Chocolate Icing over frosting; chill. Remove from refrigerator about 1 hour before serving; cut into squares.

Orange Frosting: Beat ⅓ cup softened butter or margarine and 1 teaspoon grated orange rind in a small bowl until creamy. Gradually beat in 2 cups 10X (confectioners') sugar alternately with 1 to 2 tablespoons orange juice until of spreading consistency.
Chocolate Icing: Combine 1 package (6 ounces) semisweet chocolate pieces and 1 tablespoon vegetable shortening in the top of a double boiler. Set over hot, not boiling, water until melted.

CARROT BROWNIES

Bake at 350° for 30 minutes.
Makes 32 squares.

 ½ cup (1 stick) butter
1½ cups firmly packed light brown sugar
 2 cups *unsifted* all-purpose flour
 2 teaspoons baking powder
 ½ teaspoon salt
 2 eggs
 2 cups finely grated carrots
 ½ cup chopped walnuts
 Cream Cheese Frosting (recipe follows)
 Walnut halves (optional)

1. Melt butter in large saucepan. Add brown sugar; stir until blended. Remove from heat; cool slightly.
2. Sift flour, baking powder and salt onto wax paper. Preheat oven to 350°.
3. Beat eggs into cooled butter mixture 1 at a time. Stir in flour mixture, blending well. Add carrots and walnuts, mixing well. Pour into 2 greased 8 × 8 × 2-inch baking pans.
4. Bake in a preheated moderate oven (350°) for 30 minutes or until centers spring back when lightly pressed with fingertip. Cool 10 minutes in pans on wire rack; remove from pans; cool completely.
5. Frost tops with Cream Cheese Frosting. Cut into squares and top each square with a walnut half, if you wish.

Cream Cheese Frosting: Combine 2 ounces (⅔ of a 3-ounce package) softened cream cheese with ⅓ cup softened butter in a small bowl; beat until smooth. Stir in 1 teaspoon vanilla and 1½ cups 10X (confectioners') sugar until fluffy and smooth. Makes 1 cup.

DOUBLE CHOCOLATE WALNUT BROWNIES

Bake at 350° for 35 minutes.
Makes about 24 bars.

- 1 **cup (2 sticks) butter or margarine**
- 4 **squares unsweetened chocolate (4 ounces)**
- 2 **cups sugar**
- 3 **eggs**
- 1 **teaspoon vanilla**
- 1 **cup *sifted* all-purpose flour**
- 1½ **cups coarsely chopped walnuts**
- 1 **package (6 ounces) semisweet chocolate pieces**

1. Melt butter and chocolate in a medium-size saucepan over moderate heat. Remove from heat. Preheat oven to 350°.
2. Beat in sugar gradually with a wooden spoon until thoroughly combined. Add eggs, 1 at a time, beating well after each addition; stir in vanilla. Stir in flour until thoroughly combined. Stir in 1 cup of the walnuts. Spread into a greased 13 × 9 × 2-inch pan. Combine remaining ½ cup walnuts with chocolate pieces; sprinkle over top of brownie mixture, pressing down lightly.
3. Bake in a preheated moderate oven (350°) for 35 minutes or until top springs back when lightly pressed with fingertip. Cool completely in pan on wire rack. Cut into bars or squares.

CREAM CHEESE BROWNIES

Bake at 350° for 40 minutes.
Makes 16 squares.

- 3 **tablespoons butter**
- 4 **squares semisweet chocolate (4 ounces)**
- 2 **tablespoons butter, softened**
- 1 **package (3 ounces) cream cheese, softened**
- 1 **cup sugar**
- 3 **eggs**
- 1 **tablespoon flour**
- 2 **teaspoons vanilla**
- ½ **cup *unsifted* all-purpose flour**
- ½ **teaspoon baking powder**
- ½ **teaspoon salt**
- ½ **cup chopped walnuts**
- ¼ **teaspoon almond extract**

1. Melt the 3 tablespoons butter with the chocolate in top of double boiler over hot water. Remove and cool.
2. Grease a 9 × 9 × 2-inch baking pan.
3. Blend remaining 2 tablespoons butter with the cream cheese in medium-size bowl with electric mixer until fluffy. Beat in ¼ cup of the sugar, 1 egg, the 1 tablespoon flour and 1 teaspoon of the vanilla. Preheat oven to 350°.
4. Beat remaining 2 eggs in large bowl with electric mixer until foamy. Slowly add ¾ cup sugar, beating until blended. Stir in the ½ cup flour, the baking powder and salt until smooth. Add chocolate mixture, walnuts, 1 teaspoon vanilla and almond extract.
5. Spread half of chocolate mixture evenly in prepared pan. Spread cream cheese mixture on top. Drop spoonfuls of remaining chocolate mixture on top of cream cheese. Swirl top of batter.
6. Bake in a preheated moderate oven (350°) for 40 minutes. Cool in pan on wire rack.

●●●

BROWN RICE See **RICE.**

BROWN SUGAR see **SUGAR.**

BRUNCH A hybrid meal between breakfast and lunch that combines some of the foods of each. Americans invented the meal and then created a word to describe it by using the first two letters of *br*eakfast and the last four of l*unch.* The menu possibilities are endless, but always include a fruit or juice and coffee or a hot beverage.

Most brunches are given on weekends, usually Sundays between 11 A.M. and 1 P.M. and are easy for the host or hostess to prepare. There's time on Saturday to prepare and time on Sunday to clean-up. Brunches before football games or other activities are especially popular. The hour limits the consumption of cocktails, making it easy on your budget.

Whether you've invited family or a group of friends for just a bite, or a few people for an intimate sit-down meal, consider a brunch as the ideal entertaining meal. Day-ahead or early-in-the-day preparations will give you plenty of time to spend with your guests. Here we present an international selection, although anything goes for this terrific way to start off the day!

MEXICAN BRUNCH
(Makes 6 servings.)
Margaritas or Pineapple Juice
Huevos Rancheros*
(Ranch-style Eggs)
Buñuelos* (Mexican Fritters)
Orange Avocado Salad
Mexican Hot Chocolate*

*Recipe follows

HUEVOS RANCHEROS
(Ranch-style Eggs)

Makes 6 servings.

- ¼ **cup vegetable oil**
- 6 **canned or frozen tortillas**
- 1 **large onion, diced (1 cup)**
- 1 **medium-size green pepper, seeded and diced (½ cup)**
- 1 **clove garlic, minced**
- 3 **medium-size tomatoes, peeled, seeded and diced (3 cups)**
- 1 **can (4 ounces) whole green chilies, seeded and chopped**
- ¾ **teaspoon liquid hot pepper seasoning**
- 1 **teaspoon salt**
- 6 **eggs**
- 2 **cups shredded Romaine lettuce**
- ½ **cup shredded sharp Cheddar cheese *(optional)***

1. Heat 2 tablespoons of the oil in a medium-size skillet. Heat tortillas just until limp on each side. Drain on paper toweling; keep warm.
2. In same skillet, cook onion, green pepper and garlic until tender, about 5 minutes. (Add more oil, if necessary.) Stir in tomatoes, green chilies, hot pepper seasoning and salt. Cook, uncovered, 10 minutes, stirring occasionally.
3. Heat remaining 2 tablespoons oil in a large skillet. Break and slip eggs into skillet. Reduce heat and cook slowly to desired doneness.
4. Line large serving plate with shredded lettuce. Arrange tortillas on lettuce. Slip eggs onto each tortilla; spoon sauce around eggs. Sprinkle with cheese, if using.

Overleaf: Mexican Brunch, page 105; Margaritas, Huevos Rancheros, page 105; Bunuelos, page 108; Orange Avocado Salad, Mexican Hot Chocolate, page 108

Brunch

BUÑUELOS
(Mexican Fritters)
Makes 32 fritters.

- 2 cups *sifted* all-purpose flour
- 2 tablespoons sugar
- ½ teaspoon baking powder
- ½ teaspoon salt
- ¼ teaspoon anise seeds, crushed (use a hammer)
- 1 teaspoon grated lemon rind
- 1 egg, slightly beaten
- 3 tablespoons butter or margarine, melted
- 3 to 4 tablespoons milk
  Vegetable oil
- ⅔ cup honey
- ¼ cup (½ stick) butter or margarine

1. Combine flour, sugar, baking powder, salt, anise seeds and lemon rind in a large bowl.
2. Stir in egg, butter and just enough milk to make the dough hold together.
3. Turn out on lightly-floured surface and knead 3 to 5 minutes or just until dough becomes smooth. Let rest 10 minutes.
4. Divide dough into 32 equal-size pieces. Roll each out on a lightly floured surface with a lightly floured rolling pin to a 5-inch circle (edges will be irregular). Keep between pieces of wax paper until all have been rolled out.
5. Heat about 1 inch oil in a heavy skillet to 375° on a deep-fat frying thermometer. Fry rounds, a few at a time, about 30 seconds on each side. (Buñuelos will puff up when frying.) Drain on paper toweling.
Do-ahead Tip: Buñuelos can be stored at this point between clean paper toweling in a metal tin, or frozen in single layers on a jelly-roll pan. To serve, place on a jelly-roll pan or cookie sheet in a 325° oven for 1 minute; then glaze with honey butter.
6. Just before serving, heat honey and butter in a medium-size saucepan until mixture bubbles 1 minute. Cool slightly. With a spoon, drizzle mixture over each buñuelo; let set.

MEXICAN HOT CHOCOLATE
Makes 6 servings.

- 4 cups milk
- 3 squares semisweet chocolate (3 ounces)
- 1 teaspoon ground cinnamon
- 2 eggs

1. Heat milk just to scalding in a large saucepan. Stir in chocolate and cinnamon until chocolate melts, then beat with a rotary beater until smooth.
2. Beat eggs well in a small bowl; slowly beat in about 1 cup of the hot chocolate mixture, then beat back into remaining chocolate mixture in pan. Heat slowly 1 minute, stirring constantly; beat again until frothy.
3. Ladle into heated mugs or glasses; place a cinnamon stick in each mug for a stirrer, if you wish. Serve warm.

FRENCH BRUNCH
(Makes 6 servings.)
Kir*
Strawberries with Cream
Individual Cheese Soufflés*
Herbed Tomato Halves*
Croissants
Café au Lait*

*Recipe follows

KIR
Makes 6 servings.

- 1 tablespoon crème de cassis
- 2½ cups chilled dry white wine

Combine crème de cassis and wine; stir. Pour into chilled wine glasses; serve immediately. Or serve over ice in tall glass, if you wish.

INDIVIDUAL CHEESE SOUFFLÉS
Bake at 350° for 40 minutes.
Makes 6 servings.

- 2 tablespoons butter or margarine
- ¼ cup all-purpose flour
- ½ teaspoon salt
- ¼ teaspoon pepper
- ¼ teaspoon dry mustard
- 1 cup milk
- 6 ounces sharp Cheddar cheese, shredded (1½ cups)
- 6 eggs, separated

1. Butter six 1-cup soufflé dishes or 10-ounce custard cups.
2. Melt butter in a medium-size saucepan; remove from heat. Stir in flour, salt, pepper and mustard; gradually stir in milk until smooth. Return to heat; continue cooking and stirring until mixture thickens and bubbles, 1 minute. Stir in cheese until melted. Remove from heat; let cool while beating eggs.
3. Beat egg whites until stiff in a large bowl. Beat egg yolks well in a small bowl; pour a little cooled cheese mixture into egg yolks, blending thoroughly. Then pour egg yolk mixture into cheese mixture, blending thoroughly.
4. Fold cheese mixture into egg whites until no streaks of white or yellow remain. Pour into prepared dishes, dividing evenly. Cover with plastic wrap; freeze.
5. To bake, place frozen soufflés on cookie sheet for easy handling. Bake in a moderate oven (350°) for 40 minutes or until puffed and golden. Serve immediately.

HERBED TOMATO HALVES
Bake at 350° for 20 minutes.
Makes 8 servings.

- 4 large tomatoes (about 2½ pounds)
- 2 tablespoons chopped green onion
- ¼ cup (½ stick) butter or margarine
- 1 teaspoon salt
- ½ teaspoon pepper
- ¼ teaspoon leaf marjoram, crumbled
- ¼ teaspoon leaf basil, crumbled
- 1½ cups fresh bread crumbs (4 slices)

1. Core tomatoes; cut in half crosswise. Place cut side up in shallow baking pan just large enough to hold tomatoes.
2. Sauté onion in butter in a large skillet until soft. Add salt, pepper, marjoram, basil and bread crumbs; stir with fork until crumbs are thoroughly moistened. Divide mixture evenly over tomato halves.
3. Bake in a moderate oven (350°) for 20 minutes or until tomatoes are heated thoroughly.

CAFÉ AU LAIT
The French way to serve coffee.

Pour equal parts of freshly brewed, double-strength coffee and scalded milk or light cream into heated coffee cups. Serve at once. Make a cup at a time, or in quantity.

ALL-AMERICAN BRUNCH
(Makes 4 servings.)
Cranberry Orange Punch
Egg Patty Muffin*
Granola Parfait*
Hot Coffee

*Recipe follows

EGG PATTY MUFFIN

Makes 4 servings.

2 tablespoons butter or margarine
½ small onion, diced
½ small green pepper, seeded and diced
4 English muffins, split
1 package (6 ounces) sliced boiled ham
2 eggs
4 slices process American cheese

1. Melt 1 tablespoon of the butter in large skillet. Add onion and green pepper; sauté until tender. Remove from heat.
2. Toast muffins and keep warm.
3. Cut ham into matchstick-size strips. Combine sautéed onion, green pepper, ham and eggs in large bowl.
4. Heat remaining butter in same skillet. Spoon egg mixture into 4 mounds; flatten each to make 4-inch patties. Cook until underside is set, reshaping into patty, if necessary. Turn patties; cook until bottoms are set. Place a cheese slice on each patty. Cover skillet and cook until cheese is melted. Serve in muffins.

GRANOLA PARFAIT

Makes 4 servings.

2 cups granola
2 containers (8 ounces each) vanilla yogurt
2 packages (10 ounces each) frozen mixed fruit, partially thawed and drained.

In each of 4 tall parfait glasses, place ⅛ of the granola, ⅛ of the yogurt and ⅛ of the fruit. Repeat layering. Serve immediately or refrigerate to serve later.

CHINESE BRUNCH
(Makes 8 servings.)
Chilled Mandarin Oranges
Chinese Egg Rolls*
Mu Shu Pork*
(Shredded Pork and Eggs)
Mandarin Pancakes*
Oolong or Jasmine Tea

*Recipe follows

CHINESE EGG ROLLS

These crunchy and flavorful Chinese egg rolls are superb when dipped into two pungent sauces.

Makes 12 servings.

¼ cup chopped green onions
1 small clove garlic, minced
4 mushrooms, coarsely chopped (½ cup)
¼ cup diced celery
1 tablespoon vegetable oil
½ cup fresh or frozen shelled and deveined shrimp, diced
½ package (10 ounces) frozen leaf spinach, thawed and well drained
1 can (16 ounces) bean sprouts, drained
2 tablespoons soy sauce
¼ teaspoon salt
¼ teaspoon sugar
¼ teaspoon ground ginger
1½ teaspoons cornstarch
Egg Roll Wrappers *(recipe follows)*
1 egg, beaten
Peanut or vegetable oil
Bottled Duck Sauce
Hot Mustard *(recipe follows)*

1. Sauté onions, garlic, mushrooms and celery in hot oil in large skillet for 5 minutes; add shrimp; sauté 1 minute just until shrimp turn pink.
2. Stir in well drained spinach and bean sprouts. Combine soy sauce, salt, sugar, ginger and cornstarch in small cup or bowl. Add to skillet; cook, stirring constantly until thick-ened, about 1 minute. Turn mixture into a bowl and cool completely.
3. Prepare Egg Roll Wrappers.
4. When ready to fill, spoon about 1 rounded teaspoonful or 1 level tablespoonful of filling on center of each wrapper. Brush edges with beaten egg. Bring 1 corner up and over filling, then bring each of the adjacent corners, 1 at a time, up and over enclosed filling, pressing points down firmly; roll into a neat package. Place filled rolls on cookie sheet; cover with plastic wrap.
5. Heat a 1½-inch depth of oil in electric or deep heavy skillet to 375°. Drop in rolls 8 to 10 at a time; deep-fry 2 to 3 minutes or until golden brown and crisp. Drain on paper toweling. Serve with bottled duck sauce and Hot Mustard.
To freeze rolls: Cool completely, then arrange in single layer on jelly-roll pans or cookie sheets. Place in freezer. When solid, place in plastic bags or layer in plastic boxes.
To reheat: Place egg rolls in single layer on large cookie sheet. Heat at 400° for 8 to 10 minutes.
Hot Mustard: Mix ¼ cup dry mustard with 1½ teaspoons vinegar and ⅓ cup cold water.

EGG ROLL WRAPPERS
Makes 24.

2 cups *sifted* all-purpose flour
1 teaspoon salt
1 egg
½ cup ice water
Cornstarch

1. Sift flour and salt into large bowl. Make a well in center and add egg and water. Stir with fork until dough holds together and leaves sides of bowl clean. Turn out onto lightly floured surface; knead until smooth and elastic, 5 minutes. Cover dough with bowl; allow dough to rest at least 30 minutes.
2. Divide dough in fourths. Dust pastry board lightly with cornstarch; roll each piece of dough to a 14 × 11-inch rectangle. Cut into 3½-inch squares. Stack on a plate (cornstarch will prevent them from sticking together).

Brunch

MU SHU PORK
(Shredded Pork and Eggs)

Makes 8 servings.

½ pound lean boneless pork
½ bunch green onions
5 tablespoons vegetable oil
2 cups thinly sliced or shredded Chinese cabbage
1 cup fresh mung bean sprouts
1 can (8½ ounces) sliced bamboo shoots, drained
4 eggs, beaten
1 tablespoon sesame seeds
2 tablespoons soy sauce
½ teaspoon salt
½ teaspoon sugar
Mandarin Pancakes *(recipe follows)*

1. Cut pork into match-size strips. Cut onions into 2-inch lengths, then cut lengthwise pieces into shreds.
2. Heat large, deep skillet, Dutch oven or wok over high heat. Add 1 tablespoon of the oil; swirl to coat bottom and sides. Add onions, cabbage, sprouts and bamboo shoots. Stir-fry with large metal spoon just until vegetables are wilted; remove to large bowl.
3. Reheat pan; add 2 more tablespoons oil. Add eggs, swirling pan to spread eggs into a thin layer. Cook until firm, breaking eggs into small pieces. Remove to bowl with vegetables.
4. Reheat pan; add sesame seeds and remaining oil. Add pork; stir-fry until browned and thoroughly cooked. Add soy sauce, salt and sugar. Return vegetable-egg mixture to pan. Stir-fry until heated. Serve as filling for Mandarin Pancakes.
5. Have each person fill his own pancakes. Place rounded spoonful of pork mixture in center of pancake, fold 1 side over and then fold over other side, envelope-style. Roll pancake over filling and eat with fingers, keeping open side of pancake up.

MANDARIN PANCAKES

Makes 16 pancakes.

2 cups *unsifted* all-purpose flour
¼ teaspoon salt
¾ cup boiling water
Vegetable oil

1. Mix flour and salt in a large bowl. Stir in boiling water with fork until mixture is moist. Gather into a ball. Turn out onto floured surface; knead until dough is smooth and soft, about 3 minutes. Let dough rest 10 minutes.
2. Shape dough into a roll about 16 inches long. Cut crosswise into 16 pieces. Keep pieces covered with plastic wrap while shaping.
3. Flatten 2 pieces with fingers into two 3-inch patties. Brush tops with oil, then sandwich patties with oiled tops together. Roll patties with lightly floured rolling pin from center to edges to form a thin pancake 7 inches in diameter, turning it frequently to roll both sides evenly. (Be sure not to roll edges too thinly, because you'll have to be able to separate the pancake into 2 thin layers.)
4. Repeat rolling until half is shaped. Keep pancakes stacked with wax paper between.
5. Heat a large griddle or skillet over medium heat. Cook pancakes, 1 at a time, for 1 minute on each side or until puffed in center and firm but not browned. While warm, separate each into 2 thin pancakes. Keep in plastic bag while shaping and baking remainder.
6. To make ahead, wrap in aluminum foil and refrigerate or freeze. To reheat, place in pie plate set on rack over boiling water in kettle. Cover and steam 10 minutes or until soft and hot.

——— ●●● ———

BRUNSWICK STEW This southern stew with many variations was usually made from squirrel. It is now made with chicken, corn, tomatoes and lima beans, slowly simmered to develop its delicious flavor. How it originated is not certain. Several counties in the South named Brunswick, have laid claim to originating this dish sometime around the 1820's.

BRUNSWICK STEW

Makes 6 servings.

2 bacon slices, diced
1 frying or roasting chicken (3½ to 4 pounds), cut up
OR: A rabbit of the same size
3 tablespoons flour
1½ teaspoons salt
½ teaspoon pepper
⅛ teaspoon cayenne
3 medium-size onions, sliced
1½ cups water
4 ripe tomatoes, peeled and chopped
OR: 1 can (16 ounces) tomatoes
1 red pepper, seeded and diced
½ teaspoon leaf thyme, crumbled
2 cups fresh lima beans
OR: 1 package (10 ounces) frozen lima beans
2 cups freshly cut corn kernels
OR: 1 package (10 ounces) frozen whole-kernel corn
½ pound okra, sliced
OR: 1 package (10 ounces) frozen cut okra
2 tablespoons chopped fresh parsley
1 tablespoon Worcestershire sauce

Top Stove Method:

1. Cook bacon until crisp in a large kettle or Dutch oven; remove bacon with slotted spoon; reserve.
2. Shake chicken pieces with flour, salt, pepper and cayenne in plastic bag to coat well. Brown pieces, a few at a time, in bacon drippings. Stir in onions; sauté 5 minutes. Add water, tomatoes, pepper and thyme. Bring to boiling; return all chicken pieces to kettle; lower heat; cover. Simmer 45 minutes or until chicken is almost done.
3. Add lima beans, corn, okra, parsley and Worcestershire sauce; return to boiling; lower heat; cover. Continue cooking 15 minutes longer or until vegetables are tender. Serve sprinkled with reserved bacon and additional parsley.

Slow-Cooker Method:

Cook bacon and brown chicken and onions following *Top Stove Method;* place in electric slow cooker. Add 1 cup water, tomatoes, pepper and thyme; cover. Cook on low 6 to 8 hours or until chicken is almost done. Add remaining ingredients. Cover and cook on high 25 minutes or until vegetables and chicken are tender. Sprinkle with bacon and additional parsley.

Pictured opposite: Stir-Fry Chicken Wings, page 113

Brussels Sprouts

BRUSSELS SPROUTS The sprouts are the axillary buds of a cabbage-like plant, a *Brassica,* related to cabbage, broccoli, kohlrabi, cauliflower and kale. A Brussels sprout plant grows to a height of 3 feet and will produce about 30 sprouts. The sprouts grow along the stem at the base where the leaves are attached. The leaves are pulled away to allow the sprouts to grow. Only the top leaves are left to grow.

Brussels sprouts are harvested when they are 1 to 1½-inches in diameter. The Belgians, who cultivated the plant 400 years ago, preferred Brussels sprouts that were no greater than ½ inch in diameter and exported them as a highly-prized vegetable to France. Cultivation of the plant spread to England and later to America.

Today, Brussels sprouts are a widely available winter vegetable. They're a good source of vitamins A and C, with only 36 calories in a 3½-ounce serving.

Buying and Storing: Brussels sprouts are available fresh from October through February. Look for pint cartons containing the smallest sprouts, which are dark green and firm. Yellow leaves indicate they're past their prime. Store Brussels sprouts in cartons in the refrigerator. A pint carton will make 3 servings. Frozen Brussels sprouts are also available.

To Prepare: Wash well and trim the stem ends. Remove any loose, discolored leaves. Leave sprouts whole or cut into halves.

To Cook: Place fresh Brussels sprouts in a saucepan with 1 inch boiling salted water. Cover and cook 15 minutes or until tender; drain. Season with butter, herbs, salt, pepper, ground nutmeg or buttered bread crumbs.

To Microwave: Cut large sprouts in half. Place 2 pints fresh sprouts and ¼ cup water or chicken broth in a large casserole; cover. Microwave on high power 4 minutes; stir. Microwave 3 more minutes; let stand 3 minutes; drain and season with buttered bread crumbs or a cream sauce.

BRUSSELS SPROUTS AND CHESTNUTS

Chestnuts are a nice texture foil to the leafiness of crunchy sprouts.

Makes 8 servings.

- 3 **packages (10 ounces each) frozen Brussels sprouts**
- 3 **tablespoons butter or margarine**
- 1 **can (10 ounces) water-packed chestnuts, drained**
- ¼ **teaspoon salt**
- ⅛ **teaspoon pepper**

1. Cook Brussels sprouts following label directions. Drain well.
2. Melt butter in skillet. Toss drained chestnuts in butter until heated. Add to Brussels sprouts; season with salt and pepper. Toss lightly to mix. Turn into heated serving dish.

CREAMED BRUSSELS SPROUTS AND ONIONS

Makes 8 servings.

- 2 **pints Brussels sprouts**
  OR: 2 **packages (10 ounces each) frozen Brussels sprouts**
- 1 **pound small white onions, peeled**
- 2 **tablespoons butter or margarine**
- 2 **tablespoons flour**
- 2 **cups milk**
  Salt and pepper

1. Cook Brussels sprouts and onions in boiling salted water until tender, about 15 minutes; drain; cover to keep warm. If using frozen sprouts, follow label directions.
2. Melt butter in a medium-size saucepan; stir in flour. Cook, stirring constantly, until mixture bubbles; cook 1 more minute. Remove from heat; slowly stir in milk. Return to heat; cook, stirring constantly, until sauce is thickened and bubbly, about 5 minutes. Pour over Brussels sprouts and onions, stirring gently, just to coat well; add salt and pepper to taste.

— • • • —

BUCKWHEAT Although the culinary uses and name implies a cereal or grain, buckwheat is neither a cereal nor a grain. It is an herbaceous plant that grows to a height of 8 to 20 inches. It was native to Siberia from which cultivation spread to central and northern Europe, Asia and the United States.

The triangular seeds are a staple in Russian and Polish cooking. Kasha is the Russian/Polish name for cooked buckwheat. Kasha is also used in Jewish cooking.

In Europe, buckwheat is called Saracen wheat. The seeds can be crushed for groats or ground into a flour. Much of the flour is used to make bread or blinis. Buckwheat groats are sold packaged as whole kernel, or coarse, medium or finely ground.

BUCKWHEAT CAKES

Serve these piping hot with lots of butter and maple syrup.

Makes about 40 3-inch cakes.

- 1 **cup light buckwheat flour**
- 1 **cup *sifted* all-purpose flour**
- 2 **teaspoons baking powder**
- 1 **teaspoon baking soda**
- 2 **teaspoons sugar**
- 1 **teaspoon salt**
- 2 **eggs, separated**
- ¼ **cup (½ stick) butter, melted**
- 2 **cups buttermilk**
  Butter
  Maple syrup

1. Combine buckwheat and all-purpose flours, baking powder, baking soda, sugar and salt on wax paper.
2. Beat egg yolks lightly in medium-size bowl. Stir in flour mixture alternately with melted butter and buttermilk until mixture is smooth.
3. Beat egg whites in a small bowl with electric mixer until soft peaks form. Fold into batter.
4. Drop batter by tablespoonsful onto lightly greased hot griddle; spread to 3-inch rounds. Cook on 1 side until edges begin to brown and bubbles form on surface; turn to brown second side. Serve with butter and maple syrup.

— • • • —

BUDGET MAIN DISHES Serving delicious main dishes that cost less than half-a-dollar per portion is no easy task. The trick is to buy the least expensive sources of protein (eggs, cheese, beef liver, chicken parts, turkey or tuna) and stretch them with seasonal vegetables or a grain. The result is good-tasting, protein-laden dishes at a cost per serving that's less than the price of a hamburger from a fast-food place!

STUFFED SHELLS MARINARA

Great Italian cooks have always known the art of stretching a little meat or fish into a marvelous main dish.

Bake at 350° for 45 minutes.
Makes 8 servings.

- 1 **package (12 ounces) large shell macaroni**
- 1 **can (7 ounces) chunk light tuna in oil**
- 1 **large onion, chopped (1 cup)**
- 1 **clove garlic, minced**
- 1 **can (29 ounces) tomato sauce**
- 2 **teaspoons salt**
- 2 **teaspoons leaf basil, crumbled**
- ¼ **teaspoon pepper**
- 1 **package (10 ounces) frozen chopped spinach**
- 2 **eggs**
- 1 **cup fresh bread crumbs (2 slices)**
- 1 **cup cream-style cottage cheese**
- 1 **teaspoon salt**
- ¼ **teaspoon pepper**

1. Cook macaroni, following label directions, 9 minutes; drain, reserving 1 cup of the cooking water. Place macaroni in a large bowl of cold water.
2. While macaroni cooks, drain oil from tuna into a large skillet; heat; sauté onion and garlic in oil until soft. Stir in tomato sauce, tuna, the 2 teaspoons salt, basil and ¼ teaspoon pepper; simmer 15 minutes to blend flavors. Add reserved 1 cup cooking water to sauce, if it becomes too thick.
3. Cook spinach; following label directions; drain thoroughly. Beat eggs in a medium-size bowl with a wire whisk; add cooked spinach, bread crumbs, cottage cheese, the 1

teaspoon salt and ¼ teaspoon pepper and stir until well blended.
4. Drain macaroni, 1 portion at a time, on paper toweling; fill each shell with 1 teaspoon of spinach-cheese mixture. Spoon half of the sauce into a shallow 12-cup casserole. Arrange stuffed pasta shells over sauce; drizzle on remaining sauce. Cover casserole with aluminum foil.
5. Bake in a moderate oven (350°) for 45 minutes or until shells are tender and casserole is bubbly-hot.
Note: Elbow macaroni or ziti can be substituted for shells. Spoon half the cooked pasta over sauce; top with a layer of spinach-cheese filling, remaining pasta and, finally, sauce. This recipe can be divided easily, with half spooned into a 9 × 9 × 2-inch baking dish lined with heavy-duty aluminum foil. Seal, label, date and freeze. When solid, remove foil package from baking dish. When ready to serve, peel foil from frozen pasta; place in original baking dish. Bake in a moderate oven (350°) for 1 hour.

BAVARIAN SKILLET SUPPER

Chicken hot dogs are found in the meat department, next to the regular frankfurters.

Makes 6 servings.

- 1 **package (1 pound) chicken frankfurters**
- 2 **tablespoons margarine**
- 1 **large onion, sliced**
- 1 **clove garlic, minced**
- 1 **can (29 ounces) sauerkraut, drained**
- 1 **teaspoon caraway seeds**
- 2 **tablespoons light brown sugar**
- 1 **package (10 ounces) frozen lima beans**
- ½ **cup beer or beef broth Parsley Potatoes (recipe follows)**

1. Score each frank, then cut into thirds and brown quickly in margarine in a large skillet; remove with slotted spoon and reserve. Sauté onion and garlic until soft; stir in drained sauerkraut, caraway seeds, brown sugar and lima beans and toss to coat well; place franks on top; pour beer or broth over; cover.
2. Cook over low heat 30 minutes or

until flavors are blended. Arrange Parsley Potatoes in a ring around edge of skillet.
Parsley Potatoes: Pare and boil 6 to 8 medium-size potatoes in boiling salted water in a large saucepan 25 minutes or until tender when pierced with a fork; drain water from pan. Return potatoes to heat and toss over low heat 3 minutes. Roll in ¼ cup chopped fresh parsley and arrange around skillet.

STIR-FRY CHICKEN WINGS

You can use whichever chicken parts are on special at your market.

Makes 6 servings.

- 1 **pound chicken wings**
- ½ **teaspoon salt**
- 1 **bunch green onions**
- 2 **large carrots**
- 2 **red or green sweet peppers**
- 2 **tablespoons vegetable oil**
- 1 **cup thinly sliced celery**
- 1 **cup frozen peas**
- 3 **tablespoons water Sweet-Sour Sauce (recipe follows)**
- 3 **cups hot cooked rice**

1. Cut chicken wings at each joint to separate. Sprinkle salt in a large, heavy skillet; heat; add chicken wings and brown about 5 minutes on each side; remove with slotted spoon; reserve.
2. Trim green onions; cut tops and white part into 2-inch pieces; pare carrots and cut into long, diagonal pieces; seed peppers and cut into long strips.
3. Add oil to skillet; stir-fry onions, carrots and peppers in oil; add chicken wings, celery, frozen peas and water; cover skillet and steam 15 minutes; add Sweet-Sour Sauce; cook 3 minutes. Serve with hot cooked rice.
Sweet-Sour Sauce: Combine ⅓ cup firmly packed brown sugar and 4 teaspoons cornstarch in a small saucepan; stir in 1 cup water, 1 teaspoon or envelope instant chicken broth, 3 tablespoons cider vinegar and 3 tablespoons soy sauce. Bring to boiling, stirring constantly; let bubble 2 minutes. Makes 1½ cups.

TURKEY CRÊPES WITH CHEESE SAUCE

Bake at 375° for 15 minutes.
Makes 6 servings.

- ½ cup uncooked long-grain rice
- 3 tablespoons butter or margarine
- 2 tablespoons all-purpose flour
- ½ teaspoon salt
- ¼ teaspoon pepper
- 1 cup water
- 5 tablespoons instant nonfat dry milk powder
- 4 ounces Swiss cheese, shredded (1 cup)
- 1 small onion, chopped (¼ cup)
- ¾ pound ground turkey
- ½ cup thawed frozen peas
- ¼ teaspoon leaf rosemary, crumbled
- ¼ teaspoon leaf thyme, crumbled
- ¼ teaspoon dry mustard
  Crêpes (recipe follows)

1. Cook rice, following label directions; reserve.
2. Melt 2 tablespoons of the butter in a small saucepan. Blend in flour, ¼ teaspoon of the salt and ⅛ teaspoon of the pepper; cook 1 minute. Stir water into dry milk in a small bowl until blended; stir into saucepan. Cook, stirring constantly, until mixture thickens and bubbles. Remove from heat; add cheese, stirring until melted; reserve.
3. Sauté onion in remaining 1 tablespoon butter in a large skillet until tender. Add turkey, stirring constantly, until turkey loses its pink color. Stir in cooked rice, peas, rosemary, thyme, mustard, and the remaining salt and pepper. Add ⅔ of the reserved cheese sauce, stirring until blended.
4. Spoon a heaping tablespoonful of the turkey mixture on each Crêpe; roll up. Repeat until all Crêpes are filled. Arrange Crêpes in a shallow baking dish. Spoon remaining cheese sauce over Crêpes.
5. Bake in a moderate oven (375°) for 15 minutes or until sauce is bubbly and lightly browned.

Pictured opposite: Turkey Crepes with Cheese Sauce, page 115; Vegetable-Ham Soufflé Pie, page 115; Turkey and Carrot Loaf, page 117

Crêpes: Combine 2 eggs, 5 tablespoons instant nonfat dry milk, 1 cup water, 1 cup all-purpose flour, ¼ teaspoon salt and 2 tablespoons melted margarine in the container of electric blender; whirl until smooth. Or, combine all ingredients in a medium-size bowl; beat with a whisk or beater until smooth. Refrigerate batter at least 1 hour. Heat a 7-inch skillet until hot; rub about ¼ teaspoon margarine on bottom of skillet, just to film. Pour in about 3 tablespoons crêpe batter. Tilt and turn skillet to spread batter evenly over bottom. Cook crêpe until lightly browned on bottom; turn over and brown on other side. Stack cooked crêpes with wax paper between until ready to use. Makes 12 crêpes.
Note: Crêpes can be prepared ahead and refrigerated or frozen wrapped in a plastic bag.

VEGETABLE-HAM SOUFFLÉ PIE

Bake at 425° for 10 minutes, then at 375° for 20 minutes.
Makes 6 servings.

- 1 cup sifted all-purpose flour
- ¼ teaspoon salt
- ⅓ cup vegetable shortening
- 2 to 3 tablespoons ice water
- 1 cup sliced carrots (about 4 small)
- 3 small onions, each cut into 6 wedges
- ¼ pound mushrooms, sliced (1 cup)
- 1 medium-size zucchini, cut into 2 × ¼-inch sticks
- ¼ pound cooked ham, ¼ inch thick and cut into 1-inch strips
- ½ teaspoon salt
- ¼ teaspoon pepper
- ½ teaspoon leaf marjoram, crumbled
- 3 tablespoons butter or margarine
- 3 tablespoons flour
- ¾ cup water
- 3¾ tablespoons instant nonfat dry milk powder
- 2 ounces Swiss cheese, shredded (½ cup)
- 3 eggs, separated

1. Preheat oven to 425°.
2. Sift the 1 cup flour and the ¼ teaspoon salt into a medium-size bowl; cut in shortening with a pastry blender until mixture is crumbly. Sprinkle ice water over mixture; mix lightly with a fork just until pastry holds together and leaves side of bowl clean.
3. Roll out pastry to a 12-inch round on a lightly floured surface. Fit into a 9-inch pie plate. Trim overhang to ½ inch; turn edge under; pinch to make a stand-up edge; flute. Prick shell well all over with a fork.
4. Bake shell in a preheated hot oven (425°) for 10 minutes. (Check shell after 5 minutes. If bubbles have formed, prick again.) Cool on wire rack. Lower oven temperature to 375°.
5. Cook carrots, onions, mushrooms and zucchini in boiling salted water for 5 minutes or until crisp-tender; drain. Turn into large bowl; add ham, the ½ teaspoon salt, pepper and marjoram; mix lightly.
6. Melt butter in a medium-size saucepan; blend in flour; cook 1 minute. Stir the ¾ cup water into dry milk in a small bowl; stir mixture into saucepan. Cook, stirring constantly, until mixture thickens and bubbles. Remove from heat; stir in cheese until melted. Let sauce cool while beating eggs.
7. Beat egg whites in a small bowl with electric mixer until soft peaks form.
8. Beat egg yolks until light in a medium-size bowl with same beaters. Beat in cooled cheese sauce. Measure ¼ cup of the cheese mixture; stir into vegetables. Fold remaining cheese mixture into beaten egg whites until no streaks of white remain.
9. Spoon vegetable mixture into cooled pastry shell. Carefully spoon soufflé mixture over vegetables, spreading to edge of pastry to seal in vegetables.
10. Bake in a preheated moderate oven (375°) for 20 minutes or until soufflé top has puffed and is lightly browned. Serve at once.

Buffet

TURKEY AND CARROT LOAF

Bake at 375° for 1 hour.
Makes 6 servings.

1½ **pounds ground turkey**
2¼ **cups grated carrots (about 4 medium-size)**
 1 **cup chopped fresh parsley**
 1 **small onion, chopped (¼ cup)**
½ **cup packaged bread crumbs**
 1 **teaspoon salt**
¼ **teaspoon pepper**
1¼ **cups dairy sour cream**
 1 **chicken bouillon cube**
¾ **cup boiling water**
 1 **tablespoon flour**
 2 **tablespoons dry sherry**

1. Combine turkey, 1½ cups of the carrots, ½ cup of the parsley, the onion, bread crumbs, salt, pepper and 1 cup of the sour cream in a large bowl; mix well.
2. Press ⅓ of the mixture firmly into an 8½×4½×2½-inch loaf pan. Sprinkle remaining carrots over top. Press half remaining turkey mixture over carrots; sprinkle with remaining parsley. Top with remaining turkey mixture; press down firmly. Run a metal spatula around sides of pan to loosen. Invert loaf onto greased small shallow baking pan.
3. Bake in a moderate oven (375°) for 1 hour or until golden brown. Transfer loaf to a warm serving platter.
4. Add bouillon cube to boiling water in a cup; stir to dissolve. Sprinkle flour into pan drippings; cook 1 minute. Stir in bouillon mixture. Cook, stirring constantly, until sauce thickens and bubbles. Stir a little of the hot sauce into the remaining ¼ cup sour cream in a small bowl. Return blended mixture to saucepan; stir in sherry. Cook, stirring constantly, just until sauce is hot. Add salt and pepper to taste. Slice; spoon sauce over top.

— • • • —

BUFFET The word buffet actually refers to a sideboard, cupboard or tiered table for the display of tableware. Nowadays buffet means a meal set out on a table for easy and informal food service. Many restaurants use buffet tables set near entrances to display dishes of meats, poultry, appetizers or sweets and pastries.

In Europe, buffet also means a type of fast-food restaurant found at railway stations.

If you want to serve the most fabulous foods in the greatest of style, but feel the strain could spoil the fun, the best solution is the make-ahead buffet meal. Luscious dishes can be made days ahead and heated or simply set out minutes before partytime.

SPRING BUFFET

(Makes about 16 servings.)
Chicken-Filled Pastry Boats*
Ham and Walnut Appetizers*
Springtime Lamb Ragout*
Shrimp Curry*
Condiments: Kumquats, Chopped Radishes, Shredded Coconut, Salted Peanuts
Eggplant and Pasta Salad*
Parslied Rice
Strawberry Mousse*
Fresh Strawberries

*Recipe follows

CHICKEN-FILLED PASTRY BOATS

A zesty chicken mixture fills these crispy make-ahead pastry shells.
Bake at 400° for 8 minutes.
Makes about 2 dozen.

½ **package piecrust mix**
¾ **cup finely diced cooked chicken**
 2 **tablespoons finely chopped celery**
 2 **tablespoons chopped green onions**
1½ **teaspoons finely chopped canned hot chile pepper**
½ **teaspoon lime or lemon juice**
½ **teaspoon salt**
¼ **cup dairy sour cream**
 2 **hard-cooked egg yolks, sieved Parsley**

1. Prepare piecrust mix following label directions. Roll out, half at a time, to a ⅛-inch thickness on lightly floured surface. Preheat oven to 400°.
2. Using 3-inch barquette pans or tiny tart pans, invert pans onto pastry and cut pastry ½-inch wider than pans. Press pastry into pans and trim edges even with pans. Arrange pans on cookie sheets; prick pastry with a fork.
3. Bake in a preheated hot oven (400°) for 8 minutes or until golden. Cool in pans on wire rack 5 minutes. Ease out of pans; cool completely.
4. Place in foil or plastic boxes; cover, label and freeze.
5. To serve: Combine chicken, celery, onion, chile pepper, lime juice, salt and sour cream in small bowl; toss to mix well; spoon into shells. Garnish with sieved egg yolks and small sprigs of parsley. Cover; refrigerate until serving time.

HAM AND WALNUT APPETIZERS

Bake at 400° for 10 to 15 minutes.
Makes about 36 bite-size balls.

½ **pound cooked ham, ground or very finely chopped**
½ **cup walnuts, ground or very finely chopped**
½ **cup soft bread crumbs (1 slice)**
⅛ **teaspoon ground pepper**
 1 **egg, slightly beaten**
¼ **teaspoon ground allspice Dash ground cloves**
 2 **tablespoons butter or margarine**
 3 **tablespoons red currant jelly**
 1 **tablespoon prepared Dijon mustard**
 2 **tablespoons Madeira or sherry**
 1 **tablespoon vinegar**
 2 **tablespoons walnut pieces**

1. Combine ham, walnuts, bread crumbs, pepper, egg, allspice and cloves in a medium-size bowl; blend well. Shape into 36 balls. Melt butter in 13×9×2-inch baking pan; roll ham balls in butter to coat.
2. Bake in a hot oven (400°) for 10 minutes or until browned and heated through, turning once. Cool. Place in plastic bag or freezer container; freeze up to 1 week.
3. Last minute touches: Remove ham balls to defrost (about 2 hours). Heat jelly, mustard, wine and vinegar in a small skillet until jelly is melted. Add ham balls and heat, turning often, until glazed, about 5 minutes. Serve hot; garnish with walnut pieces.

Pictured opposite: Chicken-Filled Pastry Boats, page 117; Ham and Walnut Appetizer, page 117; Springtime Lamb Ragout, page 118; Shrimp Curry, Parslied Rice and Condiments, page 118; Eggplant and Pasta Salad, page 118.

Buffet

SPRINGTIME LAMB RAGOUT

Makes 8 servings.

2½ pounds boneless lamb shoulder, cubed
¼ cup all-purpose flour
1 teaspoon leaf rosemary, crumbled
1 teaspoon salt
¼ teaspoon pepper
4 tablespoons (½ stick) butter or margarine
1 large onion, chopped (1 cup)
1 cup dry white wine
1 can (13 ounces) madrilene
24 small white onions, peeled
16 small carrots (1 pound), scraped
1 cup fresh or frozen peas

1. Shake lamb in plastic bag with flour, rosemary, salt and pepper until well coated. Heat 3 tablespoons of the butter in a large skillet. Add lamb to brown, about half at a time, turning often, until browned on all sides. Transfer pieces to a Dutch oven as they brown. Sprinkle any remaining flour mixture over lamb.

2. Add remaining butter and the onion to same skillet; sauté 5 minutes, stirring often. Stir in wine; cook, stirring and scraping browned bits from bottom of pan, 5 minutes or until reduced by half. Pour over meat.

3. Add madrilene; bring to boiling; cover. Simmer 30 minutes; add onions and carrots; simmer 1 hour longer or until meat and vegetables are tender. Remove from heat; cool. Chill overnight.

4. Last-minute touches: Remove any fat from top of stew; heat just to boiling; add peas. Cover; simmer 5 minutes longer.

SHRIMP CURRY

Makes 8 servings.

¼ cup (½ stick) butter or margarine
1 large onion, chopped (1 cup)
1 apple, quartered, cored and chopped
2 to 3 teaspoons curry powder
¼ cup all-purpose flour
2 teaspoons salt
1 cup tomato juice

1 cup water
1½ pounds cooked, shelled and deveined shrimp
2 cucumbers, pared, halved, seeded and sliced ¼ inch thick (2 cups)
½ cup plain yogurt

1. Heat butter in large skillet; add onion and apple; sauté until soft, about 5 minutes. Stir in curry powder; cook, stirring constantly, 1 minute. Blend in flour, salt, tomato juice and water. Bring to boiling; simmer, covered, 5 minutes. Cool. Spoon into freezer container; freeze up to 1 week.

2. To serve: Remove sauce from freezer; defrost several hours; heat slowly in large saucepan. Add shrimp and cucumber; heat, stirring often, until curry is piping-hot and cucumbers are just tender. Stir in yogurt. Serve with parslied rice and bowls of any of the following condiments: kumquats, chopped radishes, shredded coconut, salted peanuts or chopped green pepper.

EGGPLANT AND PASTA SALAD

Bake at 350° for 45 minutes.
Makes 8 servings.

1 large eggplant (about 1½ pounds)
1 medium-size onion, finely chopped (½ cup)
1 ripe tomato, chopped
1 clove garlic, minced
½ cup olive or vegetable oil
¼ cup lemon juice
¼ cup chopped fresh parsley
½ teaspoon leaf oregano, crumbled
2 teaspoons salt
½ pound ditalini or elbow macaroni

1. Wash eggplant; prick skin in several places with a fork.

2. Bake in a moderate oven (350°) for 45 minutes or until tender. Cool.

3. Peel eggplant; cut pulp into ½-inch dice. Combine eggplant, onion, tomato, garlic, oil, lemon juice, parsley, oregano and salt in large bowl; toss to mix well. Cover; refrigerate overnight.

4. Cook pasta in boiling salted water, following label directions. Drain. Add to eggplant mixture; toss to mix. Serve warm or cold.

5. Last-minute touches: Spoon salad into bowl lined with lettuce. Garnish with tomato, lemon and Greek or ripe olives, if you wish.

STRAWBERRY MOUSSE

Makes 8 servings.

2 pints (4 cups) strawberries
OR: 1 package (1 pound) frozen unsugared strawberries, thawed
1 envelope unflavored gelatin
½ cup sugar
½ cup water
2 egg whites
Pinch cream of tartar
1 cup heavy cream

1. Prepare a collar for a 5-cup soufflé dish: Measure wax paper long enough to encircle dish. Fold lengthwise in half (wax paper should be about 2 inches higher than rim of dish). Fasten collar with tape or string.

2. Wash, hull and pat strawberries dry on paper toweling. Puree berries, a cup at a time, in container of electric blender. Pour into bowl. Repeat until all are pureed.

3. Combine gelatin and ¼ cup of the sugar in a small saucepan; stir in water. Place over very low heat and stir constantly until gelatin and sugar are dissolved. Cool mixture.

4. Stir cooled gelatin mixture into pureed strawberries. Place bowl in pan partly filled with ice and water to speed setting.

5. Beat egg whites with cream of tartar in small bowl with electric mixer until foamy white. Beat in the remaining ¼ cup sugar, 1 tablespoon at a time, until meringue stands in soft peaks. Beat cream in another small bowl until soft peaks form.

6. Fold meringue and whipped cream into strawberry mixture until no streaks of white remain. Pour into prepared dish. Refrigerate 4 hours or until set. Remove collar gently, freeing soufflé from wax paper, if necessary, with a small knife. Garnish with additional whipped cream and strawberries, if you wish.

OPEN-HOUSE BUFFET

(Makes from 12 to 50 servings.)
Shrimp-Vegetable Mélange*
Hot Sausage and Cheese Puffs*
Fresh Dill Dip* with Raw
Vegetables
Roast Turkey Breast
with Assorted Bread Slices and
Herb Butter
Little Party Cakes*
Russian Tea Cakes*
Pacific Sparkler*

*Recipe follows

SHRIMP-VEGETABLE MÉLANGE

Makes 4 cups.

- **1 package (9 ounces) frozen artichoke hearts**
- **1 package (10 ounces) frozen cauliflower**
- **1 cup cleaned, cooked shrimp (½ pound)**
- **1 cup vegetable oil**
- **½ cup white vinegar**
- **1 tablespoon sugar**
- **1 tablespoon lemon juice**
- **1 clove garlic, crushed**
- **1 teaspoon salt**
- **¼ teaspoon dry mustard**
- **¼ teaspoon pepper**
- **⅛ teaspoon cayenne**

1. Cook and drain artichoke hearts and cauliflower separately, following label directions; drain. Place artichoke hearts, cauliflower and shrimp in a deep bowl.
2. Combine remaining ingredients in a large jar with a screw top. Cover; shake well; pour over shrimp and vegetables. Cover bowl; chill several hours, stirring occasionally. To serve, drain and arrange on a platter lined with lettuce.

HOT SAUSAGE AND CHEESE PUFFS

Bake at 400° for 12 to 15 minutes.
Makes about 50 servings (120 puffs or 2 plus per serving).

- **1 pound hot or sweet Italian sausage**
- **16 ounces sharp Cheddar cheese, shredded, (4 cups)**
- **3 cups buttermilk baking mix**
- **¾ cup water**

1. Remove sausage from casings; cook in large skillet, breaking up the meat with a fork until no longer pink, about 8 to 10 minutes. Drain off fat; spoon sausage into large bowl; cool completely. Add cheese, baking mix and water; mix with a fork just until blended.
2. Roll into 1-inch balls; place 2 inches apart on large cookie sheets.
3. Bake in hot oven (400°) for 12 to 15 minutes or until puffed and browned. Remove from cookie sheets; cool completely on wire racks.
To freeze ahead: Freeze in single layer on jelly-roll pans or cookie sheets. Place in plastic bag when frozen. To reheat: Arrange in single layer on large cookie sheet. Bake at 375° for 10 minutes.
Note: For 12 servings, use ¼ pound sausage, ¼ pound Cheddar cheese, ¾ cup buttermilk baking mix and 3 to 4 tablespoons water.

FRESH DILL DIP

A charming way to serve this dip is in a small new and well scrubbed flowerpot, surrounded by vegetables.

Makes about 2 cups.

- **1½ cups dairy sour cream**
- **½ cup mayonnaise**
- **2 tablespoons Dijon mustard**
- **⅓ cup chopped fresh dill OR: 1 tablespoon dillweed**
- **¼ cup thinly sliced green onions**
- **2 teaspoons lemon juice**
- **½ teaspoon salt**
- **¼ teaspoon pepper**

1. Combine all ingredients in a medium-size bowl and blend thoroughly.
2. Spoon into serving bowl, cover and refrigerate 1 hour or longer.
Dipper Tips: Good with raw green beans, carrot sticks, red pepper strips, any chips.

LITTLE PARTY CAKES

Bake at 350° for 25 minutes.
Makes about 50 servings (96 cakes or 1 plus per serving).

- **2 packages yellow or white cake mix**
  Water
  Eggs
- **2 tablespoons grated lemon rind**
  Apricot Glaze (recipe on page 121)
  Easy Fondant Frosting (recipe on page 121)

1. Grease a 15½ × 10½ × 1-inch jelly-roll pan. Line bottom and sides with wax paper; grease paper. Preheat oven to 350°.
2. Prepare 1 cake mix, following label directions using the water and the eggs. Stir in 1 tablespoon lemon rind. Pour batter into prepared pan.
3. Bake in a preheated moderate oven (350°) for 25 minutes or until center springs back when lightly pressed with fingertip. Cool in pan on wire rack 10 minutes. Remove from pan; cool completely. Repeat with remaining package of cake mix and remaining lemon rind.
4. Cut each cake lengthwise into 6 strips (do not separate strips). Then cut strips diagonally to make diamond-shaped cakes (48 cakes from each pan).
5. Prepare Apricot Glaze.
6. Spear each cake from the bottom with a 2-tined fork; dip in glaze, then place right side up on wire rack over a sheet of wax paper to catch drippings. Let stand until glaze is set. (Cakes can be frozen at this point.)
7. Day before serving: Prepare Easy Fondant Frosting. Pour frosting over each cake, letting excess drip down onto paper. (Drippings can be scraped into the double boiler, reheated and used). Or, spear each cake from the bottom with a 2-tined fork; quickly dip in and out of frosting; place cakes on wire rack. Let frosting set; decorate cake with contrasting frosting, if you wish.
8. Place cakes on a tray and cover loosely with wax paper. Store in a cool place.
Note: For 12 servings, use ½ package cake mix, with water and egg as label directs. Add 1 teaspoon lemon rind. Bake in a prepared 9 × 9 × 2-inch pan.

APRICOT GLAZE

Makes enough for 96 little cakes.

- **3 cups apricot preserves**
- **⅔ cup water**
- **6 tablespoons sugar**

Combine preserves, water and sugar in a medium-size saucepan. Cook over medium heat until bubbly; continue to cook 3 to 5 minutes, stirring occasionally. Pour through a fine sieve to remove any small particles.
Note: For 12 servings, use 1 jar (12 ounces) apricot preserves, 3 tablespoons water and 2 tablespoons sugar.

EASY FONDANT FROSTING

Make this recipe *twice* to frost 96 cakes.

- **8 cups 10X (confectioners') sugar**
- **½ cup water**
- **½ cup light corn syrup**
- **1 teaspoon brandy or rum extract**
  Red and green food colorings

1. Combine confectioners' sugar, water and corn syrup in top of double boiler. Set over barely simmering water. (Don't let water boil, as steam will dull frosting.) Heat, stirring often, until frosting is fluid and pourable. Remove from heat; stir in brandy.
2. Frost some of the cakes with the white uncolored frosting, then tint remainder with red food coloring and frost some of the cakes. With second batch of frosting, frost more cakes with white, then tint remainder with green food coloring.
Note: For 12 servings, use 4 cups sugar, ¼ cup water, ¼ cup corn syrup and ½ teaspoon brandy extract.

RUSSIAN TEA CAKES

Bake at 400° for 12 minutes.
Makes about 50 servings (100 cakes or 2 per serving).

- **2 cups (4 sticks) butter or margarine**
- **1 cup 10X (confectioners') sugar**
- **2 teaspoons vanilla**
- **½ teaspoon salt**
- **4½ cups *sifted* all-purpose flour**
- **1 cup ground walnuts**
  10X (confectioners') sugar

1. Beat butter with 1 cup confectioners' sugar in a large bowl until fluffy and light. Beat in vanilla and salt. Gradually blend in flour and walnuts to make a stiff dough. Preheat oven to 400°.
2. Roll dough into 1-inch balls between palms of hands. Place balls 1 inch apart on lightly greased cookie sheets.
3. Bake in a preheated hot oven (400°) for 12 minutes or until firm and lightly brown on edges. Carefully remove from cookie sheets; while still hot, roll in confectioners' sugar. Cool completely on wire racks; roll again in confectioners' sugar to make a generous white coating before serving. Keeps several weeks in tightly covered box.
Note: For 12 servings, use 1 stick butter, ¼ cup confectioners' sugar, ½ teaspoon vanilla, dash of salt, 1 cup flour and ¼ cup walnuts.

PACIFIC SPARKLER

A fruity and cooling punch.
Makes 50 4-ounce servings.

- **2 quarts orange juice, chilled**
- **2 cans (46 ounces each) unsweetened pineapple juice, chilled**
- **2 cans (6 ounces each) frozen limeade concentrate**
- **2 bottles (28 ounces each) lemon-lime carbonated beverage or ginger ale, chilled**
  Ice block or cubes
  Lime slices
  Halved strawberries *(optional)*

1. Combine orange juice, pineapple juice and limeade concentrate in large punch bowl; stir to dissolve concentrate.
2. Just before serving, add lemon-lime carbonated beverage or ginger ale. Add ice and garnish with lime slices and halved strawberries.
Note: For 12 servings, use 2 cups orange juice, 3 cups pineapple juice, ⅓ cup frozen limeade concentrate and 1 bottle (12 ounces) lemon-lime carbonated beverage or ginger ale.

— ●●● —

BULGUR Sometimes called parboiled wheat, bulgur is whole wheat that has been cooked, dried, partially debranned and cracked into coarse fragments. A convenient wheat product, bulgur makes delicious salads, soups, and is a good alternate to rice or potatoes in a menu. Bulgur is our oldest recorded use of wheat. This ancient food originated in the Near East. To rehydrate it, soak it in twice its volume of boiling water and let stand until all the water has been absorbed or until the particles are tender. Drain off excess water. Use in salads or cook with other ingredients. Store bulgur in an airtight container in a cool place and use within 6 months.

BEEF AND BULGUR

Makes 4 servings.

- **1 pound ground chuck**
- **1 large onion, chopped (1 cup)**
- **1 large clove garlic, mashed**
- **8 medium-size mushrooms (about 2 ounces), sliced**
- **¾ cup bulgur**
- **1 can (3½ ounces) chopped pitted ripe olives**
- **1 can (16 ounces) tomatoes**
- **½ cup dry sherry**
- **1½ teaspoons leaf oregano, crumbled**
- **1 teaspoon salt**
- **¼ teaspoon pepper**
- **4 ounces Muenster or Monterey Jack cheese, shredded**
- **2 tablespoons chopped fresh parsley *(optional)***

1. Cook beef slowly in a large skillet, breaking up with spoon, until beef loses its pink color. Drain off most of the fat from the skillet. Add onion, garlic and mushrooms; cook just until onions begin to soften.
2. Stir in bulgur, olives, tomatoes and their liquid, sherry, oregano, salt and pepper. Cover; simmer until bulgur is soft, about 15 minutes. (If there is not enough liquid to keep the mixture moist, add a little water.)
3. Sprinkle cheese over mixture when bulgur is almost soft. Cover and finish cooking, until cheese is melted, about 2 minutes longer. Sprinkle with parsley, if using.

Bulgur

BULGUR VEGETABLE SALAD
Makes 8 servings.

- 3 cups boiling water
- 1½ cups bulgur
- 2 small bunches green onions, sliced (1 cup)
- 2 cups shredded carrots
- 1 cup shredded zucchini
- 1 cucumber, chopped (1½ cups)
- ¼ cup chopped fresh parsley
- ½ cup white wine vinegar
- ½ cup olive or vegetable oil
- 1½ teaspoons salt
- 1 large tomato
- 4 lemon slices, halved
- 8 ripe olives
  Parsley sprigs

1. Pour boiling water over bulgur in a large bowl; let stand for about 1 hour, stirring several times until most of the water is absorbed. Drain well in a large sieve or on paper toweling; chill.
2. Add onions, carrots, zucchini, cucumber, parsley, vinegar, oil and salt to chilled bulgur; toss to mix well. Spoon salad into large salad bowl.
3. Cut tomato into 4 slices (chop the ends and add to salad); cut each slice in half; arrange on top of salad with lemon slices and olives. Garnish with parsley sprigs. Cover; refrigerate until serving time.

BULGUR CHICK-PEA SALAD
Makes 8 servings

- 1 cup bulgur
- 2 cups boiling water
- ½ cup vegetable oil
- ½ cup fresh lemon juice
- 1 cup sliced green onions
- 1 can (20 ounces) chick-peas, drained
- 1 cup finely chopped fresh parsley
- 1 cup diced carrots

1. Place bulgur in a large heatproof bowl; pour boiling water over; mix to moisten. Let stand 1 hour at room temperature. (Bulgur will expand to 3½ cups.) Drain in colander. Return to bowl.
2. Beat oil and lemon juice in a cup and pour over the bulgur; mix with a fork until bulgur is coated.

3. Place bulgur in bottom of a 2-quart glass jar with tight-fitting lid, or a bowl with cover; layer each vegetable in this order: green onions, chick-peas, parsley, carrots. Cover; refrigerate. Toss the salad to mix just before serving.

———— ●●● ————

BUN see ROLL.

BURGUNDY A region of France that produces some of the world's finest red and white table wines. It's also known for a style of cooking called *à la bourguignonne* which is the practice of braising meats in a red wine sauce with mushrooms and onions. A red Burgundy wine is full-bodied. The white Burgundies, including Chablis, are dry wines.

BURGUNDY BEEF LOAF
The robust flavor of deep red wine gives this meat loaf a classic French touch.

Bake at 350° for 1 hour and 10 minutes.
Makes 8 to 10 servings.

- 1 cup Burgundy wine
- ¼ cup finely chopped celery
- 1 clove garlic
- 1 bay leaf
- 2½ pounds ground round or chuck
- 2½ cups fresh bread crumbs (5 slices)
- 1 large onion, finely chopped (1 cup)
- 1 tablespoon chopped fresh parsley
- 2 teaspoons salt
- ¼ teaspoon leaf rosemary, crumbled
- ¼ teaspoon leaf thyme, crumbled
- ¼ teaspoon pepper
- 2 eggs
- 1 can condensed beef broth
- 1 teaspoon Worcestershire sauce
- ¼ cup water
  Burgundy Sauce (*recipe follows*)
  Chopped parsley

1. Combine wine, celery, garlic and

bay leaf in a small saucepan; bring to boiling; lower heat; simmer, uncovered, until volume is reduced to half, about 10 minutes. Remove and discard garlic and bay leaf; cool wine mixture completely.
2. Combine beef, bread crumbs, onion, parsley, salt, rosemary, thyme and pepper in a large bowl; add the wine mixture, eggs, ½ cup of the beef broth (reserve remaining broth for sauce) and Worcestershire. Mix until well blended. Shape into an oval loaf on a lightly oiled shallow baking pan.
3. Bake in a moderate oven (350°) for 1 hour and 10 minutes or until loaf is a rich brown. Remove with 2 wide spatulas to a heated serving platter; keep warm. Add reserved broth and ¼ cup water to drippings in baking pan; bring to boiling, stirring constantly to loosen browned bits. Strain into a 1-cup measure. (Add water to make 1 cup.)
4. Make Burgundy Sauce.
5. Arrange small buttered whole carrots, onions and sautéed mushrooms on platter with loaf, if you wish; sprinkle with chopped parsley. Serve with Burgundy Sauce.

Burgundy Sauce: Sauté 1 tablespoon chopped shallots or green onion in 2 tablespoons butter or margarine in a medium-size saucepan, about 2 minutes. Stir in 3 tablespoons flour; gradually add the reserved broth and ½ cup Burgundy wine. Cook, stirring constantly, until sauce thickens and bubbles 2 minutes. Stir in 1 teaspoon chopped fresh parsley. Makes about 1½ cups.

———— ●●● ————

BUTTER The history of butter traces back to Nomadic tribes who used the milk of goats, cows, ewes, mares, female asses and camels to make butter. It was quite by accident that the first butter was made when nomads carried milk in goatskin vessels on their camels, and as they traveled, the milk was jolted or churned. When the substance was tasted and liked, they deliberately made more.

Today's butter is made from the fatty substances in milk. When milk stands, these substances rise to the surface in the form of cream. Cream is then separated from the milk. When the cream is agitated or churned, the fatty globules come together into a compact mass called butter. The watery liquid exuded when butter is made is called buttermilk. The freshly churned butter is rinsed in pure water until it is homogeneous. It is left unsalted and packed into blocks or lightly salted before packing. Salt is added as a preservative.

Good quality butter should not sweat at room temperature. If it does, it contains too much water. It should smell pleasant and sweet. The color varies according to the time of year, because of the various kinds of food fed to cows at different times of the year. Butter in its natural state is nearly almost white to yellow or it can be colored with a natural yellow food coloring.

By law, butter must contain at least 80 percent butterfat and no more than 16 percent water. In addition, much of it is rated for quality by U.S. Federal graders. Butter can be salted or unsalted, and churned from sweet or sour cream. The cream from about 9 quarts of milk yields 1 pound of butter.

Butter is a source of vitamins A and D. One pat of butter (½ tablespoon) is 50 calories.

Buying and Storing: Butter is sold in ¼ pound sticks, 1 pound blocks or in cartons or tubs. Whipped butter is a form that spreads readily, even when refrigerator-cold because it is whipped to add air. It weighs less than conventional butter and is sold in sticks or in tubs. Do not substitute whipped butter for stick butter.

Store butter tightly wrapped in refrigerator. Butter absorbs other food flavors very easily. Use butter within 2 weeks or freeze, wrapped in freezer paper or heavy foil. It can be stored up to 1 month in a refrigerator/freezer or 6 months in a deep freezer at 0°F.

Butter Math
1 pound = 4 sticks = 2 cups
1 stick = ½ cup

How to Clarify Butter: Clarified butter is used not only for lobster dinners but for cooking. Clarifying is a process in which the water in the butter is evaporated and the milk particles, called casein, are precipitated to the bottom so that a golden clear fat is obtained. Foods can be fried at a higher temperature using clarified butter since there are no milk particles to cause burning. Also, spattering is greatly reduced because the water has been removed. To clarify butter, heat it in a small saucepan over low heat or use a cup in the microwave. The butter will separate into a clear yellow liquid and a white deposit. Pour off and use only the clear liquid.

MAITRE D'HOTEL BUTTER

Makes about ⅔ cup.

- **½ cup (1 stick) butter**
- **2 tablespoons finely minced fresh parsley**
- **2 tablespoons finely minced chives**
- **2 tablespoons lemon juice**

Blend butter, parsley and chives in a small bowl. Add lemon juice, a little at a time. Turn out onto wax paper; shape into a 1½-inch roll. Wrap tightly and refrigerate until firm. Cut into slices and serve 1 slice on each serving of grilled or broiled meat or poultry.

GARLIC BUTTER

Makes ½ cup (enough for 2 pounds grilled chicken, beef, veal or lamb).

Combine ½ cup (1 stick) softened butter with 1 clove crushed garlic in a small bowl. Place butter mixture on wax paper and shape into a log. Refrigerate until firm. Cut log into "pats." Place a pat of butter on each serving as it comes off the grill.

CHILI BUTTER

Makes ½ cup (enough for 2 pounds grilled chicken, beef or veal).

Combine ½ cup (1 stick) softened butter and 1 tablespoon chili powder in a small bowl; blend well. Place butter

mixture on wax paper and shape into a log. Refrigerate until firm. Cut log into "pats." Place a pat of butter on each serving as it comes off the grill.

PIMIENTO AND PEPPER BUTTER

Makes ½ cup (enough for 2 pounds grilled chicken, beef, veal or lamb).

Blot 1 tablespoon chopped pimiento and 1 tablespoon chopped canned jalapeño peppers dry on paper toweling. Combine pimiento, peppers and ½ cup (1 stick) butter, softened, in a small bowl; blend well. Place butter mixture on wax paper and shape into a log. Refrigerate until firm. Cut into "pats." Place a pat of butter on each serving as it comes off the grill.

TARRAGON BUTTER

Makes ½ cup (enough for 2 pounds grilled chicken, beef, veal or lamb).

Combine ½ cup (1 stick) softened butter and 1 tablespoon chopped fresh tarragon or 1 teaspoon crumbled leaf tarragon in a small bowl; blend well. Place butter mixture on wax paper and shape into a log. Refrigerate until firm. Cut log into "pats." Place a pat of butter on each serving as it comes off the grill.

BUTTERMILK Real buttermilk is the watery liquid extracted or drained from butter during the churning process. It is not at all similar to the commercially made buttermilk sold in one-quart cartons.

Commercially made buttermilk is called "cultured buttermilk." It is made from pasteurized skimmed or partially skimmed milk inoculated with a suitable culture of lactic acid bacteria. It is left to ferment to a thickened consistency. Sometimes salt is added.

Cultured buttermilk is a highly nutritious product with very few calories. One cup (8 ounces) has 90 calories, 9 grams of protein and is a good source of calcium and riboflavin. A dried form of buttermilk is also available.

Buttermilk can be used for beverages, cakes, breads, desserts and salad dressings.

Overleaf: Buttermilk Shrimp Soup, page 126

Buttermilk

ICED BUTTERMILK-LEMON SOUP

A quick cool soup you can put together in 10 minutes, then just chill until dinner.

Makes 6 servings.

- **2 eggs**
- **5 tablespoons sugar**
- **2 tablespoons lemon juice**
- **2 teaspoons grated lemon rind**
- **1 quart buttermilk**
  Whipped cream
  Oatmeal Crunch (recipe follows)

1. Beat eggs and sugar in bowl with electric mixer at high speed until light and fluffy, about 5 minutes. Blend in lemon juice and rind. Gradually beat in buttermilk with mixer at low speed.
2. Chill several hours. Serve in chilled soup bowls; garnish with a dollop of whipped cream and sprinkling of Oatmeal Crunch.

Oatmeal Crunch: Melt ¼ cup butter in large skillet; blend in ¼ cup light brown sugar, ¼ cup chopped almonds and 1 cup quick-cooking oatmeal. Cook over medium heat, stirring constantly with a wooden spoon, until mixture is slightly toasted and crisp. Remove from heat. Cool in skillet, stirring several times.

BUTTERMILK FRIED CHICKEN

Makes 4 servings

- **1 broiler fryer (about 2½ pounds)**
- **2½ cups buttermilk**
- **1 cup flour**
- **1½ teaspoons salt**
- **½ teaspoon leaf rosemary, crumbled**
- **¼ teaspoon pepper**
  Shortening or vegetable oil

1. Cut chicken into serving pieces.
2. Pour ½ cup of the buttermilk into a shallow dish. Combine flour, salt, rosemary and pepper in a plastic bag.
3. Dip chicken pieces in buttermilk; shake in flour mixture to coat well. Dip again in buttermilk and flour mixture to build a thick coating. Place chicken pieces on wire rack for 15 minutes to allow coating to set. Reserve remaining flour mixture.
4. Melt enough shortening, or pour enough oil, into a large heavy skillet

with a cover to ½-inch depth. Place over medium heat. When a few drops of water sizzle when flicked into the hot fat, add the chicken pieces, skin-side down. Cook slowly, turning once, 20 minutes or until chicken is golden.
5. Reduce heat; cover skillet. Cook 30 minutes longer, or until chicken is tender. Remove cover for last 5 minutes for a crunchy crust. Place chicken on a heated serving platter; keep hot.
6. Pour off all fat into a cup. Return 2 tablespoons to skillet; blend in 3 tablespoons of the reserved flour mixture; cook, stirring constantly just until bubbly. Gradually add remaining 2 cups buttermilk; continue cooking and stirring, scraping to loosen brown bits in pan, until gravy is thickened and bubbles 1 minute. Taste; season with additional salt and pepper, if you wish. Spoon over chicken.

BUTTERMILK SHRIMP SOUP

Makes 6 servings.

- **1 quart buttermilk**
- **1 package (8 ounces) frozen cooked shrimp**
- **1 cucumber, peeled and chopped (1½ cups)**
- **½ cup chopped green onions**
- **½ green pepper, seeded and chopped**
- **6 radishes, sliced**
- **1 teaspoon salt**
- **¼ teaspoon pepper**
- **1 tablespoon chopped fresh dill**
  OR: 1 teaspoon dillweed

Combine all ingredients, except dill. Cover and refrigerate at least 12 hours. Add dill just before serving.

BUTTERMILK PIE

Bake at 375° for 45 minutes.
Makes one 7½-inch pie.

- **1 7½-inch unbaked pastry shell**
- **4 eggs**
- **1¼ cups sugar**
- **½ cup buttermilk**
- **¼ cup (½ stick) butter or margarine, melted and cooled**
- **1 teaspoon vanilla**
- **1 teaspoon butter flavoring (optional)**

1. Prepare pastry shell; chill. Preheat oven to 375°. Beat eggs and sugar in a medium-size bowl with a rotary beater until fluffy. Add buttermilk and melted butter; beat just until well mixed. Stir in vanilla and butter flavoring. Pour mixture into unbaked shell.
2. Bake on lower shelf of a preheated moderate oven (375°) for 45 minutes or until center is almost set but still soft. Cool thoroughly on wire rack before slicing.

BUTTERMILK PANCAKES

Makes about 12 pancakes.

- **¾ cup *sifted* unbleached all-purpose flour**
- **¾ cup buckwheat or whole wheat flour**
- **2½ to 3 tablespoons sugar (see note below)**
- **1 teaspoon baking soda**
- **½ teaspoon salt**
- **2 eggs, slightly beaten**
- **1½ cups buttermilk**
- **2 tablespoons butter or margarine, melted**
  Butter or margarine for frying

1. Sift unbleached flour, buckwheat or whole wheat flour, sugar, baking soda and salt in a bowl. (If using whole wheat flour, add any wheat grains that remain in the sifter.)
2. Combine eggs, buttermilk and melted butter in a second bowl; gradually stir into dry ingredients just until blended, but not overmixed.
3. Heat a griddle until it is hot enough for a drop of water to sizzle. Grease with butter.
4. Using a ladle, pour about 2½ tablespoons batter onto griddle for each pancake. When edges look dry and bubbly, turn and brown second side. Serve with butter or margarine and syrup, if you wish.

Note: Vary the amount of sugar according to your family's taste.

Variation: These pancakes can be made with all-purpose flour, with or without the addition of ¼ cup wheat germ. In that case, add an extra ¼ cup buttermilk and use only 1½ tablespoons sugar and 1 tablespoon butter.

Pictured opposite: Gingered Butternut Squash, page 128

Butterscotch

BUTTERNUT A member of the walnut family, butternuts grow wild throughout the United States. The butternut and black walnut are both native to the U.S. In some sections of the country, butternuts are called white walnuts. They are not grown commercially.

Butternuts are elliptical, not round in shape. Once the outer husk is removed, the tough shell must be broken with a hammer. The kernel is then dug out with a nutpick. The rich kernels make a tasty addition to cakes, breads and cookies.

BUTTERNUT SQUASH A hard-shelled winter squash, butternut squash is beige to creamy brown and cylindrical-shaped, with a bulbous part at the end opposite the stem. They generally grow 6 to 12 inches long, and 3 to 5 inches wide.
Buying and Storing: Butternut squash is found in some markets year-round but the best time to buy it is from October to December. It keeps well at cool, dry room temperatures for several months. Each weighs from 1 to 3 pounds. Choose squash which seems heavy for its size, with no soft spots or blemishes. Plan on ½-pound squash per serving.
To Prepare: Wash and cut squash lengthwise in half. Scoop out the seeds and stringy portion.
To Cook: Butternut squash halves can be baked, boiled or steamed and then mashed. To bake, place squash, cut-side up, in a shallow baking pan; cover pan with foil. Bake in a moderate oven (350°) for 45 minutes or until fork tender. Uncover. Add butter or margarine, salt and pepper to taste. Bake 5 minutes more. Other additions: brown sugar, maple syrup, chopped nuts. To boil, place halves in a large skillet with ½ inch water. Bring to boiling. Cover and lower heat. Cook 20 minutes or until tender. Drain. Cool slightly; scoop pulp into bowl; mash or beat until smooth. Season with butter, salt, pepper and brown sugar.
To Microwave: Place halves in baking dish, cut-side down. Cover with wax paper. Microwave on high power 8 minutes. Turn cut-side up; brush with butter; sprinkle with salt, pepper and brown sugar. Microwave 2 to 7 minutes. Let stand 3 to 5 minutes.

GINGERED BUTTERNUT SQUASH
Makes 8 servings.

- **2 butternut squash (about 4 pounds)**
- **¼ cup (½ stick) butter or margarine**
- **1 tablespoon maple syrup**
- **2 tablespoons finely chopped crystallized ginger**
- **1 teaspoon salt**
- **⅛ teaspoon pepper**
- **¼ teaspoon ground nutmeg**

1. Split squash in half, scoop out seeds and membranes. Cook in boiling salted water in skillet 20 minutes or until tender; drain. Cool slightly.
2. Scoop pulp into large bowl. Add butter, syrup, ginger, salt, pepper and nutmeg. Beat with a portable electric mixer until it is well mixed.
3. Spoon into heated serving dish; keep warm.

• • •

BUTTERSCOTCH: Flavoring made from cooking brown sugar with butter. It's also the name of a popular hard candy, possibly of Scottish origin.

BUTTERSCOTCH PATTIES
Little wafers of golden butterscotch.
Makes 8 dozen 1-inch patties.

- **2 cups sugar**
- **¾ cup dark corn syrup**
- **¼ cup water**
- **¼ cup milk**
- **⅓ cup butter or margarine**

1. Lightly butter 3 large cookie sheets.
2. Combine sugar, corn syrup, water and milk in a medium-size heavy saucepan. Bring to boiling over medium heat, stirring constantly. Cook, stirring often, to 260° on a candy thermometer; add butter.
3. Cook, stirring constantly, to 280° on a candy thermometer. (A teaspoonful of syrup will separate into threads that are hard but not brittle when dropped in cold water.) Remove from heat.
4. Drop hot syrup from tip of teaspoon onto cookie sheets to form 1-inch patties; or pour into a 9×9×2-inch pan and, when almost set, mark into small squares. When firm, turn out and break apart.

BUTTERSCOTCH CRISPIES
Bake at 325° for 5 minutes.
Makes about 3 dozen.

- **1 egg**
- **¼ cup granulated sugar**
- **¼ cup firmly packed brown sugar**
- **2 tablespoons flour**
- **Dash salt**
- **½ teaspoon vanilla**
- **½ cup finely chopped walnuts**
- **¼ cup finely chopped mixed candied fruits**

1. Preheat oven to 325°. Beat egg until light in a small bowl; beat in granulated and brown sugar; stir in flour, salt, vanilla, walnuts and fruits.
2. Drop batter from tip of small spatula about 1½ inches apart, on well-greased cookie sheets.
3. Bake in a preheated slow oven (325°) for 5 minutes, or until golden.
4. Remove from the cookie sheets with a spatula; cool on wire racks.

BUTTERSCOTCH SAUCE
Makes about 1¾ cups.

- **1½ cups packed brown sugar**
- **½ cup dark corn syrup**
- **½ cup water**
- **½ teaspoon salt**
- **2 tablespoons butter or margarine**
- **1 teaspoon vanilla**

1. Combine sugar, corn syrup, water and salt in a medium-size heavy saucepan.
2. Cook over low heat, stirring constantly until sugar dissolves; stir in butter.
3. Heat to boiling; cook, without stirring, until candy thermometer reads 230°. (A fine thread spins from the end of a fork when dipped into hot syrup.) Pour into a bowl and stir in vanilla; cool. Serve warm over pudding or desserts.